WAR OF THE CENTURY

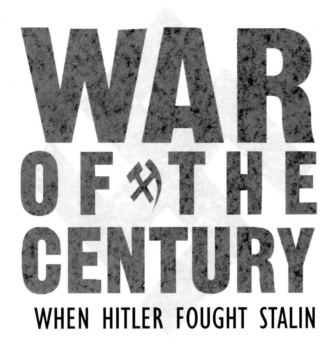

WAR OF THE CENTURY

WHEN HITLER FOUGHT STALIN

LAURENCE REES

Foreword by
PROFESSOR IAN KERSHAW

To Derek and Elisabeth Brewer

Frontispiece: German infantryman charging through a Russian forest.
Page 11: Soviet tanks, Eastern Front, 1943.

Published to accompany the television series
War of the Century first broadcast on BBC 2 in 1999.
Writer and producer: Laurence Rees

First published in 1999
© Laurence Rees 1999
The moral right of the author has been asserted.

ISBN 0 563 38477 8

Published by BBC Worldwide Ltd
Woodlands, 80 Wood Lane, London W12 0TT

Commissioning editor: Anna Ottewill
Project editor: Martha Caute
Text editor: Esther Jagger
Art director: John Calvert
Designer: Jane Parry
Picture researcher: Joanne King
Maps: Olive Pearson

Set in Palatino and Optima
Printed in France by Imprimerie Pollina s.a.
Colour separations by Imprimerie Pollina s.a.
Jacket printed by Imprimerie Pollina s.a.

CONTENTS

'The Führer says that we must gain the victory, no matter whether we do right or wrong. We have so much to answer for anyhow that we must gain the victory because otherwise our whole people...will be wiped out.'

Goebbels' Diary, 16 June 1941

'People only retain from the past what they want to find there.'

Adolf Hitler, 25 October 1941

FOREWORD

When Hitler's aggression eventually pushed Europe into war in 1939, it was not the war he had wanted. Since the 1920s he had envisaged fighting a war in the East, against the Soviet Union, against the enemy which he saw as 'Jewish Bolshevism'. He had wanted British support for his Eastern war. Instead, he found himself forging a pact with the Soviet Union, his ideological enemy, and at war with Great Britain, his would-be ally. But Hitler never meant the pact with Stalin to last. Within weeks of defeating France in 1940, he had already turned his sights on destroying the Soviet Union. At the end of March 1941 he instructed his generals to prepare, in the coming fight against Bolshevism, to carry out a 'war of annihilation'.

The invasion of the Soviet Union on 22 June 1941 was the start of a war such as the world had never seen before. It was a war, as Hitler said it would be, utterly different in character from that in Western Europe, a war of unparalleled genocidal barbarity which unleashed the Holocaust against the Jews, and left at its end a death toll of over 30 million. A titanic clash of two ruthless dictatorships whose ferocious ideological conflict had emerged from the conditions left by World War I, it determined more than any other theatre of hostilities the outcome of World War II. And it shaped the face of Europe in a Cold War lasting for a subsequent 45 years. It was truly the war of the century.

Yet it is surprising how little even now is known in the West about this war. Not unnaturally, the emphasis here is heavily placed on the war fought by the British and American allies – the Battle of Britain, the Blitz, the desert war, the war in the air, the Battle of the Atlantic, D-Day, and the liberation of Western Europe. All, of course, were essential and heroic contributions to the eventual Allied victory. And it is right that they are seen as that. But, by contrast, the war on the Eastern Front – the epicentre of World War II – has suffered relative neglect. This book helps to remedy that deficiency. The demise of the Soviet system opened up access to new material that Laurence Rees's book, and the television series on which it draws, were able to exploit for the first time. The eye-witness testimonies assembled in both series and book – perhaps the last moment it was possible to have done so – highlight both the policy decisions that cost the lives of millions, and the experiences of ordinary men and women on both sides – those inflicting suffering, and those who suffered – in the war of the century. This testimony graphically evokes the horrifying atmosphere of this war, and allows us access to the mentalities that made such unimaginable barbarity possible.

I wish the book the wide readership it deserves.

Ian Kershaw
Professor of Modern History
University of Sheffield

INTRODUCTION

I first made a film in the Soviet Union in 1989 in the distant days of Communist rule. Almost everywhere I went I had a government 'minder' at my shoulder. As a result, the Russian interviewees all spoke in propaganda slogans and I used none of their comments in the finished programme. Only our ability to interview expatriate nationals who could talk without restraint saved the project from disaster.

I thought of that experience in 1998 in the depths of the Belorussian countryside whilst I listened to a woman describing how, brutal as the German occupiers had been during the war, the local Soviet partisans had been crueller still – an opinion that would have landed her in jail had she expressed it when the Communists were still in power. Now there was no minder, no propaganda, no convenient version of the past. She had the opportunity, for the first time in her life, to speak freely about her personal history.

Travelling across the former Soviet Union, we heard fresh and extraordinary stories about the war wherever we went. They ranged from the ethnic Kalmyk who told us how, despite winning a Soviet medal for bravery, he was snatched from the Red Army by Stalin's secret police because he was the 'wrong' nationality, to the female member of SMERSH who talked with relish of shooting an unarmed German prisoner in the back of the neck; from the farmer forced by the Nazis to clear a suspected minefield by walking over it, to the Soviet secret policeman who brutally restored order in Moscow in October 1941.

In high-rise flats in Moscow, in shacks on the Russian steppes, in hamlets in the remotest parts of the Ukraine, we interviewed people whose personal experiences would have been dismissed as wild in the extreme had they been contained within the pages of a novel. Collectively their stories built into an impressionistic picture of a war so brutal, so unconcerned with the suffering of the innocent, so phenomenally unjust, as to haunt the memory of all of us who listened to them speak. A vision of the world emerged from their testimony that was cold, arbitrary and without redemption. In the face of it, all sense of the democratic ideal of individual justice had to be abandoned.

It remains hard for those of us who have been brought up with the folk memory of the war against Hitler in Western Europe to appreciate the difference in kind between the two wars – in the West and in the East. One German Panzer officer, who fought in both theatres of war, told me that compared to the fighting on the Eastern Front, the war against the British and the Americans had been a 'holiday'. He was not making a joke.

In the war in the East both sides were guilty of appalling crimes. Stalin's cynicism and paranoia meant that no one was safe from him or his secret police. Hitler's contempt for the compassionate ideals of religion and the protection afforded by the rule of law was such that, whilst as a general rule he wanted to see duelling banned, he wished it could still be permitted between priests and lawyers. On the Eastern Front his desire was to see the enemy obliterated. His plans for Moscow were simple – he wanted the Soviet capital turned into a gigantic lake.

Of course, neither this book nor the television series on which it is based are a substitute for detailed accounts of the conflict, and inevitably much is omitted. No book of this length could pretend to cover the entire war – least of all a book like this, whose claim to originality rests upon unique personal interview material. But what the techniques of journalism can add to our understanding of the past is a human dimension which is sometimes missing from a scholarly account. I remember a history professor whose field was the French Revolution saying to me, 'My biggest regret is that I can't know what it was like to actually be there.' Now television (and consequently this book), in questioning, challenging and recording the memories of victims, bystanders and perpetrators, can preserve first-hand experience for ever.

This is not a happy story and it offers little comfort. But it should be taught in our schools and remembered. For this is what human beings were capable of in the twentieth century.

LAURENCE REES
London, May 1999

CHAPTER 1

HIGH HOPES

I n the whole of history there has never been a war like it. In its scale of destruction the war on the Eastern Front was unique; from Leningrad to the Crimea, from Kiev to Stalingrad, the Soviet Union was devastated – at least 25 million Soviet citizens died. And in the end what did the German aggressors have to show for it? A broken, divided country which had lost much of its territory, and a people burdened with the knowledge that they had launched a racist war of annihilation and, in the process, spawned the cancer of the Holocaust.

But at the time there were many people – and not just Germans – who thought that the decision to invade the Soviet Union was a rational act in pursuit of German self-interest and, moreover, that this was a war the Germans would win.

In the summer of 1940 Adolf Hitler, despite his swift and dramatic victory over France, faced a major military and political problem. The British would not do what seemed logical and what the Führer expected – they would not make peace. Yet Hitler was frustrated by geography – in the shape of the English Channel – from following his immediate instincts and swiftly crushing the British just as he had the French. Hitler did order preparations to be made for an invasion of England, but he was always half-hearted in his desire to mount a large seaborne landing. Germany, unlike Britain, was not a sea power and the Channel was a formidable obstacle. Even if air superiority could be gained, there remained the powerful British Navy. And there was another, ideological, reason why Hitler was not fully committed to invading Britain. For him, it would have been a distraction. Britain contained neither the space, nor the raw materials, that he believed the new German Empire needed. And he admired the British – Hitler often remarked how much he envied their achievement in subjugating India. Worse, if the Germans let themselves be drawn into a risky amphibious operation against a country Hitler had never wanted as an enemy, every day the

OPPOSITE Adolf Hitler in 1941, the year he felt 'spiritually free' (as he wrote to Mussolini) as a result of invading the Soviet Union.

potential threat from his greatest ideological opponent would be growing stronger. (It was just ironic that he was not yet at war with this perceived enemy, since in August 1939 Germany and the Soviet Union had signed a Non-Aggression Pact.)

All this meant that, from Hitler's point of view, there was an alternative to invading Britain: he could invade the Soviet Union. Both Hitler and his military planners knew that Germany's best chance of victory was for the war in Europe to be finished swiftly. Hubert Menzel was a major in the General Operations Department of the OKH (the Oberkommando des Heers, the German Army headquarters), and for him the idea of invading the Soviet Union in 1941 had the smack of cold, clear logic to it: 'We knew that in two years' time, that is by the end of 1942, beginning of 1943, the English would be ready, the Americans would be ready, the Russians would be ready too, and then we would have to deal with all three of them at the same time.... We had to try to remove the greatest threat from the East.... At the time it seemed possible.'

Germany's need for new 'living space' (*Lebensraum*) had been a recurring theme in Hitler's early political testimony. And he had always been clear about where Germany should find its new empire. Famously, he had written in *Mein Kampf* in 1924: 'We are taking up where we left off six hundred years ago. We are putting an end to the perpetual German march towards the south and west of Europe and turning our eyes towards the east.... However, when we speak of new land in Europe today, we must principally bear in mind Russia and the border states subject to her. Destiny itself seems to wish to point the way for us here.'

And then there was the political motive. Hitler, in one of the typically stark (and false) choices he posed the German people, had maintained that if Nazism did not prevail, the evil of Bolshevism would engulf Germany. And ever since the days of the left-wing take-over of Munich in 1919 – the Räterepublik (the councils' republic) – the fanatical German right wing had believed that Bolshevism and Judaism went hand in hand. Nazi propaganda trumpeted that not only had many of the leading figures in the Räterepublik been Jewish, but so had many of those behind the Russian Revolution. By the time Hitler came to power in 1933 the words 'Jewish' and 'Communist' were almost synonymous to his followers.

Hitler was deeply prejudiced about the Soviet Union – this one country became the particular focus for his anti-Semitic, anti-Communist, anti-Slav beliefs. He would describe Moscow as the headquarters of the 'Judaeo-Bolshevist world conspiracy'. He believed profoundly that the Soviet Union was the greatest threat to Germany. In a private memorandum written in 1936 he stated: 'Germany will, as always, have to be regarded as the focus of the Western world against the attacks of Bolshevism.' In public, in a speech at the Nuremberg rally in 1937, he referred to the leaders of the Soviet Union as 'an uncivilized Jewish-Bolshevik international guild of criminals' and called the Soviet Union 'the greatest danger for the culture and civilization of mankind which has ever threatened it since the collapse of the states of the ancient world'.

Associated with this overwhelming ideological hatred of the Soviet Union was a more concrete fear: Hitler was concerned about the higher birth-rate of the Slavs. He remarked that they were 'an inferior race that breed like vermin'. Hitler foresaw grave danger if eventually the Soviet Union became a 'modern' nation with a vastly larger population than Germany's. To eliminate the need for future conflict – on less advantageous terms – Germany had to act swiftly.

None of that, however, meant that Hitler was driven to war with the Soviet Union by a kind of myopic fanaticism. He had already shown that he was perfectly prepared to put aside his deeply held beliefs when it was politically expedient. That was the reason Ribbentrop, the Nazi Foreign Minister, had flown to Moscow in August 1939 to conclude the Non-Aggression Pact with the Soviet Union. Out of simple political necessity Germany needed to secure its Eastern border in the light of Hitler's desire to invade Poland in the very near future. 'What has happened to the principles of *Mein Kampf*?' a British newsreel of the time balefully commented. Pragmatism had happened: that was the answer.

On 31 July 1940 it was once again pragmatic – not ideological – considerations that were voiced by Hitler at the Berghof, his mountain retreat in southern Bavaria, when he met with his military commanders. Yes, he believed that an invasion of Britain should be considered – air attacks would begin as soon as possible – but the whole enterprise remained fraught with risk. Now, logically, he was driven to another possible way of finishing the war. Hitler asserted that, since Britain's hopes were kept alive by the thought that the Soviet Union was still out of the war and might one day come to its aid, the destruction of the Soviet Union would shatter Britain's last reason to continue the war.

It's hard to accept now, given today's relative balance of armed forces between Britain and Russia, but at the time the Germans gave every impression of being more frightened of the British – with their mighty fleet and empire – than the Soviet Union. So when, at that meeting on 31 July, Hitler voiced his intention to crush the Soviet Union, there was no evidence that his military commanders were appalled by the news. Just like Hitler,

HITLER'S EUROPE

Germany

German-Soviet demarcation line 8 September 1939

area annexed by USSR 1939

area occupied by Germany by May 1941

Axis Powers and satellites

area or country collaborating with Axis Powers

unoccupied or neutral country

NORWAY

North Sea

DENMARK

REP. OF IRELAND

UNITED KINGDOM

London

NETHERLANDS

Hamburg • Elb

Brussels •

BELGIUM

RHINELAND (re-occupied 1936)

G E R

LUXEMBOURG

Frankfur

Seine

Paris •

FRANCE

SAARLAND (to Germany by plebiscite 1935)

Rhine

Munich

ATLANTIC OCEAN

VICHY FRANCE

SWITZERLAND

R h n

ITALY

Corsica

PORTUGAL

SPAIN

Sardinia

0   300 km

M e d i t e r r a n e a n

they seem to have thought at the time that a land war against the Soviet Union was preferable to a seaborne invasion of Britain.

The context of that meeting is important. As Hitler gathered with his military leaders, they were flushed with a remarkable victory over France. In numbers there had not been much to choose between the two sides, and yet under Hitler the German Army had crushed the French in six weeks. This would have been a major achievement on its own, but set against the background of the disastrous way in which the German advance had bogged down far short of Paris in the trenches of World War I, the spring 1940 victory must have seemed phenomenal. Any war against the Red Army would be conducted using the same apparently unstoppable Blitzkrieg tactics of swift motorized attack that had just proved so successful in France; as Hitler put it, this was a new type of war which would be 'unbelievably bloody and grim', but it would always be 'kindest because it will be the shortest'.

As the Soviet Marshal Georgy Zhukov later put it: 'The German forces invaded the Soviet Union intoxicated by their easy victories over the armies of Western Europe...and firmly convinced both of the possibility of an easy victory over the Red Army and of their own superiority over all other nations.'

Hindsight allows us to condemn the military judgement of these men who so fatally underestimated the warlike capacity and will to fight of the Soviet Union. The war on the Eastern Front has come to seem uniquely insane; the act of a single power-crazed individual who held his generals in thrall. What act could be more guaranteed to fuel the unquenchable fire of the dictator's ambition and more certain to destroy his nation in the end? That is certainly the easy explanation that Franz Halder, one of the military commanders closest to Hitler, gave after the war. Halder, who was Chief of the Army General Staff between 1938 and 1942, spoke during his de-Nazification (and in an interview in the 1960s) of a meeting he had had with the Commander-in-Chief of the German Army, Walter von Brauchitsch, at the end of July 1940. Halder described how Brauchitsch asked him, 'Have you ever thought about [attacking] the East?' Halder said he replied, 'That fool [Hitler]. I honestly believe he will even get Russia on to us. I won't even think of preparing anything for it.' What could be more understandable than this response? By telling this story, Halder positions himself as just another of the mad Führer's victims.

But there's a problem with Halder's convenient version of history – it doesn't stand up to scrutiny. On 3 July, weeks before the meeting with Brauchitsch, Halder revealed in his private war diary that he had already floated with his planners the idea of a campaign against the Soviet Union, a 'military intervention' which would 'compel Russia to recognize Germany's dominant position in Europe'. Halder had decided on this action

himself, without any direct order from Hitler. Like all of those who wished to survive and prosper in the high reaches of the Nazi state, Halder had learnt that it wasn't sufficient simply to follow orders – they had to be anticipated.

Nor are Halder's actions in the early days of the German campaign in the East those of a sceptic. On 3 July 1941, just 12 days into the war, Halder wrote in his diary: 'It is thus probably no overstatement to say that the Russian campaign has been won in the space of two weeks.' That same day he wrote to one of his colleagues, Luise von Benda (who later married General Alfred von

Hitler and his generals. Franz Halder, Chief of the Army General Staff, is on the far right.

Jodl, see page 28), also voicing the view that the Soviet Union had all but lost the war; he added that Hitler had come round to his quarters to chat and congratulate him on his birthday, and had stayed for an hour at teatime. 'I will keep this day as precious in my memory,' writes the clearly euphoric Halder.

The temptation to alter the past must have been overwhelming for Halder – after all, no general wishes to go down in history as playing a significant part in the greatest defeat his country has ever suffered. It is this all too human desire to rewrite history that has fuelled over the years the popular myth that the only proponent of the German invasion of the Soviet Union in 1941 was one power-crazed lunatic. It was simply not so.

Part of the reason for the Germans' over-confidence was contemptible then and is still so now. The Nazis believed that the inhabitants of the Soviet Union were racially inferior – from its planning stage this was to be no ordinary war, but a racial war of annihilation against a 'sub-human' people. They also thought that the whole Jewish/Bolshevik system they saw in place in the Soviet Union was rotten and would crumble in the face of the expected early military losses of the Red Army. But there were other, more rational, reasons why they (and many of the Allies) thought that the Soviet Union was scarcely capable of putting up a fight.

Along with the rest of the world, Hitler and his military commanders had watched the effect of Communist rule on the Soviet Union's military capacity. And the Germans were encouraged by what they saw, for they believed that the Soviet leader Josef Stalin had, during the 1930s, substantially weakened the Red Army. Stalin's character, which would help shape and define the course of the forthcoming war in the East, was, in the eyes of the Nazis, devastatingly flawed.

Unlike Hitler, who had essentially created the Nazi Party, Stalin had not been the vital driving force behind Soviet Communism – that role had fallen to Lenin. Hitler's charismatic authority was irreplaceable in the Nazi Party – he never had a serious rival. Stalin was a black hole of charisma, a fixer, a *praktik*, a 'man who got things done', the silent figure at the back of the room who waited, listened and was underestimated until the moment came. Amongst the leading Communists he had seemed least likely to succeed Lenin in 1924; Zinoviev and Trotsky were more gifted speakers, Bukharin more engaging. Even after he became leader of the Soviet Union, Stalin remained a man of the shadows. He made but a small fraction of the number of personal appearances that Hitler did during the 1930s. Paradoxically, this worked in Stalin's favour – the image was created that he was always working for the Soviet Union, hidden but watchful. Yet at the annual parade in Red Square Stalin looked out not just on his own portrait but on Lenin's as well. Stalin was constantly reminded that he was the follower – and followers can be replaced. As Bukharin once said: Stalin 'is unhappy because he cannot convince everyone, even himself, that he is greater than everyone, and this is his unhappiness....'

Stepan Mikoyan grew up in the Kremlin compound in the 1930s. His father Anastas was a leading member of the Politburo and he himself met Stalin on many occasions. 'Stalin was by nature very attentive,' says Mikoyan, 'and he watched people's eyes when he was speaking – and if you didn't look him straight in the eye, he might well suspect that you were deceiving him. And then he'd be capable of taking the most unpleasant steps.... He was very suspicious. That was his main character trait.... He was a very un-principled man.... He could betray and deceive if he thought it was necessary. And that's why he expected the same behaviour from others...anyone could turn out to be a traitor.'

The later Communist leader Nikita Khrushchev put it this way: 'All of us around Stalin were temporary people. As long as he trusted us to a certain degree, we were allowed to go on living and working. But the moment he stopped trusting you, the cup of his distrust overflowed.' Trotsky, who always felt himself Stalin's superior, gave this judgement on the new Soviet leader: 'Being enormously envious and ambitious, he could not but feel his intellectual and moral inferiority every step of the way.... Only much later did I realize that he had been trying to establish some sort of familiar relations. But I was repelled by the very qualities that would strengthen him...the narrowness of his interests, his pragmatism, his psychological coarseness and the special cynicism of the provincial who has been liberated from his prejudices by Marxism but who has not replaced them with a philosophical outlook that has been thoroughly thought out and mentally absorbed.'

This, of course, was an underestimation of Stalin. He might not have possessed Trotsky's charisma, but Stalin was the more politically astute; his combination of natural intelligence, pragmatism, suspicious nature and ruthlessness enabled him to develop an extremely effective way of retaining power: terror. The Nazis took careful note of how, during the 1930s, Stalin eliminated anyone whom he, or his secret police, the NKVD, thought presented the remotest threat.

As a consequence, Stalin specialized in using fear as a factor of motivation. One historian describes it as 'negative inspiration' – the idea that his followers had constantly to prove themselves to him. It was foolhardy in the extreme to criticize the system in front of him. One young Air Force general boldly stated, at a meeting at which Stalin was present, that the number of accidents in military planes was so high because 'we are forced to fly in coffins'. Stalin replied: 'You should not have said that, General,' and had him killed the following day.

From 1937 Stalin presided over the purging of the Red Army. Thousands of its most senior officers were tried and executed in an atmosphere of paranoia. Mark Gallay was a Soviet test pilot who lived through this horror. 'In 1937 the conditions in our country were oppressive,' he says. 'There was the heavy atmosphere of the Stalinist repressions. It concerned everyone:

OVERLEAF Stalin and Lavrenti Beria, who, as People's Commissar for Internal Affairs, was to become the feared head of the secret police. This picture was taken on a holiday in Stalin and Beria's native Georgia.

scientists, the military, and amongst the military the Air Force. Suffice to say that, within the space of a few years, the head of the Air Force was changed many times. One after the other, they were repressed and eliminated.' Gallay explained how he led a 'dual existence' during this time. On the one hand he was starting his career, courting his future wife, 'in the prime of my youth', someone who would set off for work each day with 'pleasure'. On the other, as a candidate-member of the Communist party, two or three times a week he would attend sinister meetings. 'And we tried to pick someone at random from our own milieu and to get him to talk about his links with "enemies of the people".... But the vast majority of people were innocent. And at these meetings someone would make a speech. Well, you know, there is a breed of person who likes to give a condemned man that final push. Someone would get up to make a speech because they were forced to do so. The majority maintained a gloomy silence. And they knew that if they voted to exclude someone from the party, he would be arrested that night.'

This charge of 'enemy of the people' was an extremely effective device for the security forces; few allegations could appear at first sight more serious, and yet the actual details of the offence remained vague. Lavrenti Beria, the head of the NKVD, is said to have quoted the theory, which he assigned to Stalin, that 'an enemy of the people is not only one who makes sabotage, but one who doubts the rightness of the party line. And there are a lot of them among us, and we must liquidate them.'

This policy of terror did not even spare those who were valuable to the military machine. On a 'dank and cold' October day in 1937, Mark Gallay arrived at the aerodrome to witness a chilling sight. The tailplanes on the aircraft in front of his hangar were being painted over. Each experimental plane carried the initials of its designer, and now the painters were obliterating 'A.N.T.' – the mark of one of the most gifted aero-engineers of the time, Andrei Nikolaevich Tupolev. Gallay realized that Tupolev must have been arrested; that the very man who had designed the new war-planes had just become 'an enemy of the people'.

An insight into the way Stalin wished the secret police to deal with these 'enemies of the people' is contained in this instruction sent to local NKVD authorities: 'The Central Committee...authorizes the use of physical coercion by the NKVD beginning in 1937. It is well known that all bourgeois intelligence services use physical coercion of the most disgusting kind against representatives of the socialist proletariat. The question therefore arises why socialist organs should be more humane towards the rabid agents of the bourgeoisie and sworn enemies of the working class and collective farms?'

It is not hard to guess the effect such arbitrary arrests, torture and murder had on the morale of the Soviet military – particularly in areas such as experimental plane design, an environment in which progress can be made only through trial and error. 'Naturally,' says Mark Gallay, 'when the general atmosphere is oppressive, it does not facilitate the flourishing of initiative.... Under the conditions of the Stalinist terror, everyone was afraid of making mistakes.'

Goebbels recorded Hitler's view of Stalin's purges in 1937: 'Stalin is probably sick in the brain,' said Hitler. 'Otherwise you can't explain his bloody regime.' For Hitler himself had practised nothing like this. On the contrary, when he came to power he had initially worked with the generals who were already in place. Even when, in the late 1930s, he had been presented with an opportunity to remove those military figures who were still not enthusiastic about Nazism, he had merely forced the wavering generals into retirement – they had been given not a bullet in the head but a pension.

Stalin did more than purge the Red Army to confirm to the Nazis that he was 'sick in the brain'. Even his own family fell victim to his obsessive paranoia. Two of his brothers-in-law were arrested and shot, two of his sisters-in-law were arrested and imprisoned. A third brother-in-law, Pavel Alliluyev, died of suspected poisoning after going to work in the Kremlin one day in November 1938. 'That was his character,' says Kira, Pavel Alliluyev's daughter and Stalin's niece. '"Stalin" – it means "steel".' (Born Iosif Dzhugashvili, he had adopted a pseudonym, like many Communist agitators, in his case Stalin – 'of steel'.) As Kira explains, 'He had a heart of steel.... It would seem that Stalin had hinted to someone that Papa had to be got rid of because he was continually compromising him [Stalin] by getting him to set people free. And obviously Stalin got fed up with it.... Of course, he knew that he couldn't arrest my father. He wouldn't be able to prove to my mother that he was an enemy of the people. So he got rid of him.'

Kira and her family spent time at Stalin's dacha in the country, where she marvelled at the other side of his character. 'He was very fond of my younger brother – he called him "mushroom", he would sit him on his knee and chat to him affectionately.... And I could say that I didn't want to eat something or that I didn't like something. He'd say: "Leave her alone! If she doesn't want to, then she doesn't have to!"'

But after her father's death, Kira and her mother's relationship with Stalin changed. 'He became very strange. He kept us at a distance. We no longer saw him after 1939... The way we lived after Papa had been poisoned, it was like something out of a Shakespearean tragedy.' Kira and her mother were both imprisoned, though neither of them could see the reason why. 'A normal person would think, how is it possible to destroy your own family? But his power was greater than anyone else's. He was clearly above everyone else. He didn't see anything around him, he just wanted everyone to say "Yes" to everything he did. Anyone who said "No" or who doubted anything would be made an "enemy of the people". His enemy.... My whole life was destroyed. My husband left me

because his parents said to him: "They'll put you in prison too!" I married again but it was too late the second time...it was too late to have children. My life was really destroyed. But what should I do about it? I decided to be an optimist. So I go on living. You can't go back and change things.'

Of course, terrible as these stories of personal suffering are, they would have given the Nazis no concrete reason to be certain that Stalin had so damaged the Soviet Union that the country would collapse under the German attack. Even today there is argument about the extent to which the purges alone harmed the Red Army. For the Soviet military machine was also weakened by its chaotic expansion in the years preceding the war when inexperienced officers were thrust upwards in the hierarchy into positions for which they had little training (a situation, of course, exacerbated by the purges). While during 1937–8 more than 30 per cent of officers were expelled from military service, only in recent years have the original Western estimates of officers *arrested* during the same period dropped from between a quarter and a half of the total number to well below 10 per cent. But what the argument about numbers fails to do is recognize the harm done to the morale and initiative of the Soviet armed forces by the knowledge that the merest error could result in arrest or even execution.

Indeed, as Hitler and his generals began in the summer of 1940 to assess how the Red Army might fight in the forthcoming war, they had more compelling evidence than knowledge of the purges to make them feel optimistic about the conflict ahead. Nine months before, in November 1939, the Red Army had attacked Finland. Stalin had planned to take the country forcibly into the

Finnish troops during 1939–40. Lightly armed, and knowing how best to use their forest-covered countryside, they gave the Soviets a lesson in guerrilla warfare.

Soviet Union as the Karelo-Finnish Soviet Republic. On paper the Finns appeared to have little hope. They faced a numerically stronger Soviet force – one estimate says the Red Army had nearly a three-to-one advantage. But it didn't work out the way Stalin desired. 'It was a terrifying scene,' says Mikhail Timoshenko, who fought on the Soviet side with the 44th Ukrainian Division in the Finnish War. 'It gave you the impression that someone had intentionally sent our people to freeze to death. There was no enemy visible anywhere. It was as if the forest was doing the shooting all by itself.'

The Red Army received a lesson in how a small, motivated and lightly armed force could conduct effective guerrilla war. 'In small groups, of say 10 or 15 men, the Finns were sneaking up to our bonfires, firing short bursts from their machine guns and then immediately running away again...when we sent our men to follow the tracks that we'd observed in the snow, they didn't return. The Finns lay in wait for them and killed them all in ambush. We realized that it simply wasn't possible to wage war against the Finns.' As a result of failures in tactics, leadership, equipment and communications, Timoshenko's division began to fall apart. By February 1940 they were down to 10,000 men – less than half strength. 'Personally, I thought that there had been some kind of misunderstanding – the decision made no sense to me. Why had they sent our division there when there was no enemy, when it was so dreadfully cold, when people were freezing to death?' Out of his regiment of 4000 only about 500 escaped from Finland unharmed. The Soviet system dealt with this failure in a familiar way. The 'guilty' commanders were shot. In Timoshenko's case, both his regimental commander and commissar (see page 31) were executed. A peace treaty was finally signed with Finland in March 1940. By sheer superiority of numbers the Red Army had gained some territory – but at the terrible cost of 130,000 Soviet dead.

Even a committed Communist like Mikhail Timoshenko realized the message being sent to the Soviet Union's fellow signatory of the Non-Aggression Pact: 'The Germans, naturally enough, came to the conclusion that the Red Army was weak. And in many respects they were right.' The German General Staff examined the Red Army's tactics in the Finnish War and reached a simple but damning conclusion: 'The Soviet "mass" is no match for an army with superior leadership.'

All this goes some way to explain why, on 21 July 1940, nearly two weeks before the major military conference at the Berghof, Hitler went so far as to ask General Alfred von Jodl, Chief of the Operations Staff of the High Command of the Armed Forces (OKW), if the German Army could move into action against the Soviet Union that autumn. Jodl rejected the idea of attacking so soon; there wasn't enough time to complete the necessary planning. Instead, preparations were begun that summer for an attack the following year.

The formal directive for the invasion of the Soviet Union was issued on 18 December 1940. Up to then the codenames Otto and Fritz had been used for the operation, but Hitler now renamed it Barbarossa after the nickname of Emperor Frederick I, who, according to ancient belief, would rise again to aid Germany when the country needed him most.

As 1940 came to an end, all the various strands of Hitler's thinking must have confirmed him in his view that this giant undertaking was the right way forward. On a practical level, the failure of the Luftwaffe in the Battle of Britain had destroyed any chance of a successful German invasion of England – so how else could Britain and the USA be neutralized except through the elimination of their potential ally on the European continent, the Soviet Union? On a political level, the visit of Soviet Foreign Minister Vyacheslav Molotov to Berlin in November 1940 had demonstrated to Hitler the dangerous way in which the Soviet Union wished to exploit the Non-Aggression Pact. Had not Molotov announced that the Soviet Union wanted to annex part of Romania? On an economic level, Germany was hugely dependent on the Soviet Union for raw materials with which to fight the war – suppose at a crucial moment the Soviet Union simply turned off the tap? On an ideological level the Communists were, of course, loathsome to Hitler and the Nazis. Wouldn't the Führer feel 'spiritually free' (as he later wrote to Mussolini) by breaking the Non-Aggression Pact, this marriage of political convenience? On a military level, what more evidence did the German Army need of their own innate superiority than to compare their own swift subjugation of the French with the inability of the Red Army to crush the puny Finns?

Not until the beginning of 1941, after the timing and objectives of Barbarossa had been laid down, were any practical doubts voiced. The head of the Wehrmacht's Office for Armament Economy, General Thomas, now raised with the High Command some of the difficulties that the German Army would face during the invasion – how would they be supplied with sufficient fuel and provisions inside Soviet territory? At a meeting with Hitler on 3 February, Halder mentioned these problems and suggested ways of overcoming them (the idea that the German Army might 'live off the land' and loot the resources of the Soviet Union to augment any deficiencies in supply was optimistically put forward by the Wehrmacht's central economic agency; see page 60). A later, more devastating, assessment, again from General Thomas, of the logistical challenge that the German Army would face was probably never even shown to Hitler.

That February another flaw in the invasion plan was discussed, albeit briefly. Barbarossa was not intended to be an invasion of the whole Soviet Union. The Germans would stop at the Ural Mountains, leaving the Soviets to retreat beyond – to the forests and swamps of Siberia. Not even Hitler thought he had the military power at his disposal to march east to the Pacific Ocean. (As Hubert Menzel, a Panzer division officer, put it: 'This was Blitzkrieg – but without borders.') Field Marshal von Bock, who was to command Army Group Centre (the military thrust charged with advancing along the central Minsk–Smolensk–Moscow axis), asked how, after the defeat of the Red Army, the Soviets would be 'forced to make peace'. Hitler replied vaguely that 'after the conquest of the Ukraine, Moscow and Leningrad...the Soviets will certainly consent to a compromise'.

Despite all this, the confidence of some in the German High Command remained overweening: 'The Russian colossus will be proved to be a pig's bladder,' said General Jodl. 'Prick it and it will burst.' Perhaps Jodl was thinking of the humiliation the generals had suffered when their pessimistic assessment of the German Army's chances against the French had proved so wrong. This time, the generals would not be accused of being 'negative'.

During that spring Hitler made changes to the OKH's three-pronged invasion plan. He thought their emphasis on the need to push on to Moscow was misplaced. Central to Hitler's conception of the forthcoming hostilities was his belief that this was a new kind of war, a war of destruction, and it was more important that the enemy's forces be eliminated in vast encirclement battles than that their capital be taken. Hitler's change of emphasis was accepted without protest. His expectation was clear – the Red Army would be surrounded and eliminated far west of Moscow and then the country would collapse because of the loss of its industrial capacity.

That spring key decisions were also taken about the manner in which the invasion should be conducted. To Hitler and the Nazis, the Soviet Union was not like France or Belgium or any other 'civilized' country in the West. From the beginning, this was viewed as a war against savages who carried within them the dangerous, corrupting belief of Communism infested with Judaism. Halder, reflecting Hitler's desires, noted on 17 March 1941 that 'The intelligentsia put in by Stalin must be exterminated' and that 'In Great Russia force must be used in its most brutal form.' Hitler did not hide from his generals his view that this was to be a war of 'annihilation' – he said as much to them in a speech on 31 March. They, in turn, did not resign or protest, as these views were codified in a series of orders which set the letter and spirit in which the war was to be fought. These orders, which were labelled 'criminal' at the Nuremberg trials after the war, were prepared not by the SS but by the legal arm of the Army's own High Command.

The first 'criminal' order was the Barbarossa-Decree, under whose terms partisan fighters were to be shot out of hand and collective reprisals against whole communities were authorized. This was followed by the infamous Commissar Order, which called on soldiers to shoot Soviet political officers – the commissars. (For much of its life the Red Army operated under 'dual command', with the professional military officers having to consult political commissars before issuing substantive orders. One of the great fears of the early revolutionaries had been that the Army might one day move against the Communist Party – the presence of the commissars ensured this could not happen.)

It is hard today to understand how the modern army of a cultured people like the Germans could have accepted that they were about to fight a war outside international convention – a war in which they were expected to be not just soldiers but murderers. But to meet Bernhard Bechler is to comprehend the mentality of the time that made it possible. He wasn't just a soldier who accepted the contents of the Commissar Order – he was one of the people who signed it. Acting as ADC to General Müller, a 'General for Special Tasks' in the Army High Command, he signed to witness the signature of Field Marshal von Brauchitsch. 'I was proud of the fact that my name was on the order,' says Bechler. 'But back then one shouldn't think of it as a special event. There were

Bernhard Bechler, whose signature appears on the infamous Commissar Order of 1941 – a fact that made him 'proud'.

20, 30 events happening at the same time and this is just one of them... Insights never come until after the fact. Afterwards, when I realized its significance, what a dirty business it actually was, yes. But at the time one didn't really notice much of it.'

In so far as he did stop to think about it, Bechler felt that 'at the time we were still convinced that there would be a victory. And if we had won, everything would have been right. You must not forget that. If we had won the war against the Soviet Union, none of this, not even the crimes or whatever, would have mattered.'

When pressed harder on the ethical question – the sort of moral standards he was working to in issuing such orders – Bechler replied: 'If I believe that there is a danger for the Western world, that the Soviet Union is a threat to civilization, if this is what I believe and embrace, I take a moral stance. I am morally obliged to prevent this, and my morals prompt me to avail myself of means which I wouldn't have used otherwise – in order to prevent Bolshevism prevailing in Europe.... One didn't see it as a crime against the Russian people because Hitler had said: "There is no such thing as a crime on the part of the Germans." This was simply our moral stance: they had to be destroyed. The potential had to be destroyed, everything that kept the system going.'

Bernhard Bechler's response, with its convoluted logic, is significant. It represents the same reasoning process that Heinrich Himmler, Reichsführer SS, used in order to justify the killing of Jewish children. In essence it amounts to: 'The threat to our society from these people in the future is so great that in this case the end justifies the means.' By such reasoning do intelligent people justify their most bestial acts. It shows that sophistication and culture are no bar to atrocity – indeed, they can be an aid, for once the intelligent mind devises a justification, there is no limit to the consequent brutality.

The German Army had already seen how the Einsatzgruppen – the special 'task forces' charged with liquidating the Nazis' ideological enemies under Reinhard Heydrich, Head of the Main Reich Security Office – had operated in Poland against Jews and the Polish intelligentsia. There had been complaints from some German generals about the resultant killings, but they had been contemptuously dismissed. Hitler had remarked that 'you can't make a war with Salvation Army methods'. Nearly two years on, the German Wehrmacht – and especially its more ambitious members – knew that brutality was to be expected. But this wasn't a case of just 'putting up' with a war of annihilation. The Army and its High Command knew they had to compete with Himmler's SS for a role in the future Great German Empire. If they were perceived as 'weak', they would later be brushed aside. After the conquest of the Soviet Union, only those military leaders who showed 'ideological purity' could hope to receive the Führer's blessing.

Not everyone in the German Army went along with the 'criminal' orders. But the majority of German Divisions did enforce them. The forthcoming war was presented to them not only as a 'crusade' against a brutal, savage enemy, an attempt to bring civilization in the form of a German empire to the East, but also as a struggle that seemed to be a military and economic necessity – if it was lost, then Germany was lost. Such circumstances made it easier for them to understand why this had to be a war without rules. As Goebbels recorded in his diary of 16 June 1941: 'The Führer says that we must gain the victory no matter whether we do right or wrong. We have so much to answer for anyhow that we must gain the victory because otherwise our whole people...will be wiped out.'

The Germans set about assembling the force of 3 million men that would invade the East, and inevitably Stalin learnt of the new troop concentrations. But what should he make of this intelligence? Was this just a provocation – a means of ensuring that the Soviet Union did not interrupt the flow of raw materials to the German war machine? Or was it more serious – did it mean war? One of those Soviet agents who did learn the true reason behind the German military build-up was Anatoly Gurevich, head of Soviet military counter-intelligence in France and Belgium. Established with a cover as a South American company director, he managed to infiltrate himself into a circle of German commanders in Belgium. In October 1940 Gurevich learnt that the Germans planned to attack the Soviet Union the following year. 'I started to find out how the troops were moved,' he says, 'and that they were being transferred to the Eastern Front.' By the beginning of 1941, Gurevich recalls, he was sending messages to Moscow via the Soviet embassy in Brussels that 'the war had to start in May 1941'. Richard Sorge, the Soviet agent in Japan, sent messages to Moscow to much the same effect.

Stalin's attitude can be gleaned from a secret document released only since the fall of Communism. Dated 16 June 1941, it was sent by the People's Commissariat for State Defence of the USSR, V. N. Merkulov, and reads: 'A source working in the German Aviation Headquarters reports: 1. Germany has concluded all necessary measures for war in preparation for an armed assault against the USSR and an attack can be expected at any moment... In the Ministry for the Economy they are saying that at a meeting of all the economic planners destined for the "occupied" territories of the USSR, Rosenberg [who was shortly to be appointed Minister for the Occupied Territories by Hitler] also made a speech, stating that "the very notion of the Soviet Union must be wiped off the map".' Across the front of this report Stalin has scrawled: 'Comrade Merkulov, you can send your "source" from his position on the staff of the German Air Force to his fucking mother. He is not a "source" but a disinformant.'

Stalin has often been berated for not taking warnings such as these more seriously. But, once more, it's easy to mount such criticisms once the end result is known. At the time, it can't have seemed so clear-cut. As Stalin would have seen it, Hitler's prime concern was Britain, and invading the Soviet Union would have committed Germany to a war on two fronts. Furthermore, the Soviet Union was keeping to its various agreements with Germany to provide raw materials for the Nazi war effort. In October 1939 the Soviet Union had even let the German Navy use an ice-free port east of Murmansk to repair its U-boats for the war in the North Atlantic. Why would Hitler want to jeopardize this fruitful relationship?

On 10 May 1941 Rudolf Hess, Hitler's Deputy, had parachuted into Scotland. What prospects did this conjure up in Stalin's mind? Were the British and the Nazis colluding with each other? If they were, this was good reason to ignore the British intelligence information he was now receiving, which claimed there would be a German invasion. Perhaps the British were trying to force the Soviet Union into a foolish strike against Germany so as to let themselves off the hook. The British, remember, had been less than enthusiastic about an alliance between themselves and the Soviet Union in 1939.

Stalin considered all these possibilities against the background of his overwhelming desire to do nothing to provoke the Germans. A war against the Nazis in 1941 would not have been in his interests. It is likely that he thought the Soviet Union could not escape an eventual conflict against the Germans, but he felt that this war would not come until 1942–3 at the earliest. In the meantime he could prepare his army and benefit from the secret protocol of the Non-Aggression Pact with Germany which gave the Soviet Union increased territory in Europe – including a large portion of Poland. So a part of Stalin's determination to believe that there was no definite plan to invade the Soviet Union must have been wishful thinking – what seemed a good idea to the Germans would have seemed a very bad idea indeed to Stalin.

Stalin was not alone in believing that appeasing Hitler would enable the Soviet Union to escape invasion. Marshal Zhukov, appointed Chief of the Soviet General Staff in February 1941, later said, 'Most of the people around Stalin supported him in the political judgements he made before the war, especially the notion that, as long as we did not rise to any provocation, or make any false step, then Hitler would not break the Pact and attack us.'

It is against this background that one should judge the claims, which have emerged since the fall of Communism, that the

OPPOSITE Stalin – as inscrutable as ever. While Hitler often looks at the camera in a 'great man' stare, Stalin remains cold and distant.

Soviet Union itself was planning a strike against the Germans in 1941. (This was also the claim that Hitler and the Nazi propagandists made immediately after the invasion to justify their attack – although there is no evidence that they actually believed it when they were planning the invasion.) Such hard evidence as has emerged essentially revolves around one Soviet document, dated 15 May 1941, entitled 'Considerations for planning the strategic deployment of the Soviet Union's Armed Forces in the event of war with Germany and its allies'.

A study of the complete document reveals that it is far from being the 'smoking gun' that justifies the conspiracy theorists in claiming that Stalin was planning an imminent attack on Germany. The context of the document makes it clear that it is written in response to the information reaching the Soviet military that the German Army is massing on the borders of the Soviet Union: 'The situation, in the current political climate, suggests that Germany, if it were to attack the USSR, would be able to raise against us as many as 137 infantry divisions, 19 tank divisions, 15 motorized divisions, 4 cavalry divisions and 5 landing aircraft divisions – a total of 180 divisions...' The report goes on to talk of the probable direction of the main thrust of the German attack 'south of Demblin' and that 'This attack will, in all likelihood, be accompanied by an attack in the north from East Prussia against Vilna and Riga, as well as a short, concentrated attack from around Suvalki and Brest against Volkovysk, Baranovichi.'

After listing the possible route of the German attack, the report suggests that 'we should attack the German Army when it is still at the deployment stage and has not yet had time to organize the front and co-ordinate the different arms of the service'. Two counter-offensives are then suggested into German territory.

A careful reading of the report shows that it represents not a plan for an unprovoked attack on Germany but a response to German mobilization and an attempt to frustrate a possible invasion. It is also evident that far from being a secret plan kept hidden until that moment, the document is the last in a series of deployment plans – a contingency in the event of invasion from the West.

Despite the popular myth that the Soviets did nothing to prepare for a possible German attack, the truth is that the leaders of the Red Army did consider in detail how their forces should be deployed – the only problem was that they deployed them in the wrong way. The basic military assumption that the 15 May document, and those that preceded it, rested upon was that in the event of war the Red Army should practise 'active defence'. Instead of using the vast depth of the Soviet Union to soak up the enemy,

Stalin believed that large portions of the Red Army should be positioned right against the frontier, ready for a massive counter-attack into enemy territory.

Stalin's behaviour in the spring of 1941 is that of a man desperately trying to do nothing to antagonize the Germans, rather than that of a warlord waiting to strike. (The Russian historian Professor Viktor Anfilov states that Marshal Zhukov told him that Stalin did see the 15 May document and reacted angrily: 'Are you mad? Do you want to provoke the Germans?') And newly declassified documents confirm that the Soviet Union was still honouring its deliveries of raw materials to Germany up to the moment of the invasion.

Just because Stalin had no desire to invade Germany at this time, it doesn't mean, of course, that had the war gone on he would have felt his Pact with the Nazis was sacrosanct. But Stalin's natural caution made him wary of over-committing himself. He did not break his neutrality treaty with Japan until after the Americans dropped their first atomic bomb. Only then did Stalin order the Red Army to invade Japanese-held territory in China and rush towards Japan itself. In parallel, then, one can posit a scenario in which Stalin would first have waited to see how the war in the West progressed and then, if he could have moved in the endgame to the benefit of the Soviet Union, no treaty would have prevented him.

This is, it is worth remembering, exactly the reason why the Germans felt they needed to eliminate the threat from the Soviet Union so quickly. Both Hitler and Stalin knew that time favoured the Soviet Union. To this limited extent, then, not just the Nazi leadership but many former German soldiers still consider this a preventive war: 'I don't want to claim that Hitler waged a preventive war in the sense of forestalling a looming attack,' says Rüdiger von Reichert, then an artillery officer with Army Group Centre. 'You can use the term "preventive war" only in so far as saying that he [Hitler] knew that the conflict was necessary, and that he was in a more favourable position if he launched an attack first, and that he had to take into account that Stalin might launch an attack too. So in this way there was sympathy for the decision to attack Russia.'

The original plan for Operation Barbarossa had called for an attack in May 1941, but this start date could not be met because in March a military coup in Belgrade had overthrown the Nazi ally Prince Paul. As a result, on 6 April German troops invaded Yugoslavia. For strategic reasons Hitler ordered them to carry on into Greece. The Italians had botched their own invasion of the country some months earlier, and

OVERLEAF German soldiers cross the River Bug into Soviet-held territory on 22 June 1941. This bridge was just one of hundreds of different crossing points.

Hitler could not risk the German Army's southern flank being exposed during Barbarossa. Both Yugoslavia and Greece swiftly fell to the German Blitzkrieg and the war was over by the end of April. But because of these unforeseen military actions Barbarossa could not be launched until June.

Hitler himself, as the Eastern campaign fell around him in 1945, was to blame the eventual German failure in the Soviet Union on the delay in implementing Barbarossa. Whilst there was some confusion caused by the swift redeployment of German units back into their start positions for Barbarossa, it was a particularly wet spring and the likelihood is that the invasion date would have been in June regardless. In any event, it was not the matter of a few weeks' delay that spelt doom for Operation Barbarossa, but a fundamental miscalculation about the true nature and difficulty of the task ahead.

Certainly none of the German veterans we spoke to felt at the time that Barbarossa was going to fail because it was launched in June rather than May. On the contrary, many were filled with optimism about the ease of the task ahead. On the morning of the attack Bernhard Bechler went to his sister's to say goodbye – he was about to travel to Hitler's new advance headquarters in East Prussia: 'I said, "Listen, we will part now. In a few weeks I'll ring you from Moscow." ...I was utterly convinced that this would happen, and I was in fact proud of our plans.'

Just before dawn on Sunday 22 June 1941 Rüdiger von Reichert, as an artillery officer with the 268th infantry division, waited to cross the border into Soviet-held Poland. 'The situation was made so grotesque because approximately an hour before a brightly lit, peaceful train had driven by, destined to go to our then ally who was about to be attacked.' At half past three they attacked 'with a huge burst of fire, and on the demarcation line opposite the guards were shot down'. For Wolfgang Horn, a soldier in the 10th Panzer Division, the massive artillery barrage that signalled the opening of the war gave him 'a great feeling about the power being unleashed against the dubious and despisable [sic] enemy'.

The Germans moved forward in three great thrusts along an invasion front of 1800 kilometres, the longest in history – Field Marshal von Leeb with Army Group North aiming for the Baltic states and Leningrad, von Bock with Army Group Centre attacking towards Minsk, Smolensk and eventually Moscow, and von Rundstedt with Army Group South heading into the Ukraine.

Though the Soviet defenders were roughly equal in numbers of fighting men to the German invaders (just over 3 million on each side), they were little match for them. A combination of their weak deployment close to the border (based on the military doctrine of 'defence through attack' which did not allow effective defensive operations), lack of training, inexperience of their commanders, and inadequate military hardware (much of which was outdated or in need of repair) meant that the Soviet forces were easy prey for the encirclement tactics of the Germans.

The invaders had elevated their Blitzkrieg attack to a new level of tactical deftness. Conventional military theory had asserted that armoured attack should be in waves – first bombers, then artillery, then tanks, then motorized infantry and so on. But under General Heinz Guderian, Commander-in-Chief of Panzer troops and the man whose original thinking about armoured warfare had made successful Blitzkrieg possible, the Germans had revolutionized that approach. Instead their tanks, dive bombers and artillery all focused simultaneously on one narrow point in the enemy line – sometimes no wider than a single road. This level of coordination was possible only because of both sophisticated communications – spotters inside the forward tanks would radio back the exact position that the artillery batteries should shell – and extensive previous battle experience. 'We were well trained in it,' says Wolfgang Horn. 'We had done it in France – when breaking through to the port of Calais, for example. So we knew how to attack as a spearhead, regardless of what was on the sides...it was a very coordinated attack, always.'

Once the Panzers had burst through the enemy line, they forced their way on, leaving the following infantry to plunge through the gap and encircle the bewildered opposition. In the early days of Barbarossa it was Army Group Centre that had most success with this tactic, swiftly advancing to Smolensk deep inside the Soviet Union. But Blitzkrieg tactics had not been designed for such an enormous country and in the vast distances involved the conventional infantry could not keep up with the Panzer advance, so the spearheads had to stop and wait for them.

But these were problems of success, and from the individual German soldier's point of view the early weeks of Barbarossa were essentially days of glorious victories. 'You thought it was a doddle,' says Albert Schneider, a soldier in the 201st Assault Gun Battalion. 'The Russians will all defect in droves or will be taken prisoner and detained in a camp somewhere.' The ease of the initial advance made him think 'we will have a splendid life and the war will be over in six months – a year at most – we will have reached the Ural Mountains and that will be that.... At the time we also thought,

OVERLEAF German armoured vehicles advance into Soviet-held territory in June 1941. The central plains of the Soviet Union were a perfect battleground for the sophisticated German Blitzkrieg.

goodness, what can happen to us? Nothing can happen to us. We were, after all, the victorious troops. And it went well and there were soldiers who advanced singing! It is hard to believe but it's a fact.'

On the morning of 22 June Stalin was awoken at his dacha at Kuntsevo just outside Moscow when Marshal Zhukov, then Chief of the General Staff, telephoned him with the news of the invasion. Initially Stalin thought there must have been a mistake – perhaps there had been a coup and Hitler's generals had taken over, or perhaps this was just another provocation. Stalin ordered the Foreign Ministry to ask the Japanese to help – maybe they could mediate with the Germans. Stepan Mikoyan's father was summoned to a crisis meeting that morning at Stalin's office in the Kremlin. Then, and for the first few days of the war, 'nobody understood what was going on...communications had been disrupted. It wasn't clear where our army was or where the Germans were.'

'I fought on the border for three days and three nights,' says Georgy Semenyak, then a 20-year-old soldier in the Soviet 204th Division. 'The bombing, shooting...explosions of artillery gunfire continued non-stop.' On the fourth day his unit began to retreat – into chaos. 'It was a dismal picture. During the day, aeroplanes continuously dropped bombs on the retreating soldiers.... When the order was given for the retreat, there were huge numbers of people heading in every direction – although the majority were heading east.' As he trudged east through Belorussia, Georgy Semenyak watched in despair as his officers deserted. 'The lieutenants, captains, second-lieutenants took rides on passing vehicles...mostly trucks travelling eastwards.' By the time his unit approached Minsk, capital of Belorussia, his section was left with 'virtually no commanders. And without commanders, our ability to defend ourselves was so severely weakened that there was really nothing we could do.... The fact that they used their rank to save their own lives, we felt this to be wrong. But every man has his weaknesses.'

Blame should not be unqualified for those officers who deserted their men. For by the time of the German invasion in 1941, one estimate is that, as a result of the purges and the hasty expansion of the Red Army, about 75 per cent of officers and 70 per cent of political officers had been in their jobs for less than a year.

Stalin's actions, in those early days of the war, bore little relation to the reality on the battlefield. He berated his generals and called for advances into enemy territory, action in pursuit of the original Soviet plan of counter-attack – a plan now utterly unrealistic in the face of German advances of up to 60 kilometres on the first day of Operation Barbarossa.

OPERATION BARBAROSSA

FINLAND

Helsinki

Lake Ladoga

Gulf of Finland

Tallinn

Narva

Leningrad

Baltic Sea

ESTONIA

Novgorod

Kalinin

Riga

LATVIA

Moscow

Memel

LITHUANIA

Dvina

Vitebsk

Vyazma

ARMY GROUP NORTH (Leeb)

Königsberg

Kaunus

Vilnius

Orsha

Smolensk

EAST PRUSSIA

Mogilev

Tula

ARMY GROUP CENTRE (Bock)

Minsk

USSR

Vistula

Bialystok

BELORUSSIA

Warsaw

Brest-Litovsk

Pripet

Kursk

GENERAL GOVERNMENT (POLAND)

Bug

Pripet Marshes

ARMY GROUP SOUTH (Rundstedt)

Kiev

Kharkov

Lvov

Dnieper

Donets

Vinnitsa

UKRAINE

SLOVAKIA

Carpathian Mts

Dniester

HUNGARY

Odessa

Front lines 1941

June 21

September 1

September 30

German attack

furthest limit of German advance December 1941

Sea of Azov

Crimea

ROMANIA

Sevastopol

Bucharest

Black Sea

0   300 km

As Hitler saw the early German successes, he must have felt confirmed in his belief that the Red Army would be destroyed within weeks. And he was not the only one, as the invasion began, to have little faith in the Soviet capacity to resist. The US Secretary of the Navy wrote to President Roosevelt on 23 June: 'The best opinion I can get is that it will take anywhere from six weeks to two months for Hitler to clean up on Russia.' Hugh Dalton, the British Labour politician, recorded in his diary on 22 June: 'I am mentally preparing myself for the headlong collapse of the Red Army and Air Force.' Just before Barbarossa had been launched, the British Joint Intelligence Committee had stated that in their judgement the Soviet leadership lacked initiative and the Red Army had 'much obsolete equipment'. The British War Office told the BBC that they should not give out the impression that Russian armed resistance would last more than six weeks.

A crisis occurred in Moscow on 27 June when Stalin and other members of the Politburo attended a meeting at the Commissariat of Defence on Frunze Street. Stepan Mikoyan's father was there: 'They began asking Zhukov questions and they realized that the military were almost totally in the dark. They couldn't tell them anything: where the army was...where our army was...where the Germans were...how far they'd advanced.... Nothing was clear. Zhukov was so shaken up that, as my father described it, he was on the verge of tears.' Stalin was now aware that the Germans were about to take Minsk – and the Red Army could do nothing to prevent it. He stormed out of Frunze Street, saying: 'Lenin founded our state and now we've fucked it up.' Shortly after the meeting he left for his dacha – and stayed there.

In Germany, Goebbels had been concerned about how the public would react to news of the invasion. He had been the one who had read out Hitler's proclamation at 5.30 a.m. on 22 June, stating that the war was necessary to 'counter this conspiracy of the Jewish-Anglo-Saxon warmongers and the equally Jewish rulers of the Bolshevik headquarters in Moscow'. Maria Mauth, then a 17-year-old schoolgirl, recalls hearing her father react to the news of the invasion in the way Goebbels must have feared: 'I will never forget my father saying: "Right, now we have lost the war!"' But then, as the accounts of the first easy successes arrived, the attitude changed. 'In the weekly newsreels we would see glorious pictures of the German Army with all the soldiers singing and waving and cheering. And that was infectious of course. We thought about it in those terms and believed it for a long time, too. We simply thought it would be similar to what it was like in France or in Poland – everybody was convinced of that, considering the fabulous army we had.'

The early days of the invasion – the middle of July 1941. The broad mass of Soviet tanks were no match for the Germans.

The fact that Germany was attacking a country with which it had signed a Non-Aggression Pact made little difference. It was the Pact itself that had been the aberration. Now Germans could voice once more their comfortable prejudices about the nature of the hordes who lived on their Eastern borders. 'Russian history had always been barbaric,' says Maria Mauth, 'and we now thought, well, there must be something to it – just look at them! And everybody said: "Gosh, just look at them! Right, well, that's not a life worth living!" Those were the actual words. That was the image of the Russians, and on top of that they were cowardly too, because they had retreated so quickly.'

Germans like Maria Mauth didn't form their views about the Russians out of fear of denunciation if they failed to spout these prejudices – she is a sincere woman who at the time believed that 'We were not like them. We were much better.' The propaganda newsreels confirmed her view that the 'Russians' were 'ugly, under-developed.

ABOVE German troops enter Minsk in July 1941. The flag on the rear of the armoured vehicle helped prevent casualties from friendly fire.

OPPOSITE A German soldier enjoys a haircut in Minsk in 1941. The building displays the hammer and sickle, but also flies the SS flag.

Sometimes they were shown with faces like apes, with huge noses, no hair, in rags, filthy – well, that was the image, so you said to yourself, well, God, OK, why not?'

Such sentiments as these were widespread not just amongst German civilians but throughout the army as well, and helped ensure that this war did not just begin as a brutal racist war but escalated from there. On the battlefield, in those early days of the war, Walter Schaefer-Kehnert, an artillery officer in a Panzer division, found his belief confirmed that these 'Russians' – as the Soviet people were most often referred to by the Germans – were 'more stubborn, more primitive, less civilized'. 'When they counter-attacked and we had to leave the wounded behind and

then we came back again, we found all the wounded had had their heads split open with short infantry blades. Now you can imagine our soldiers, when you see your wounded friend has been brutally killed, then they were furious.'

Another reason why the war in the East was so 'different' from the one in the West was the murder away from the battlefield. According to plan, the Einsatzgruppen began their terrible work in the very first days of the war. They immediately killed, amongst others, 'Communist party officials and Jews in the service of the party or state' – a definition that was interpreted in the widest sense.

'Jewish-Bolshevism, you see, that was the big enemy,' confirms Carlheinz Behnke, then a soldier in the SS-Panzer Division Wiking. 'And these were the people to fight against because they meant a threat to Europe, according to the view at the time.... And the Jews were simply regarded as the leadership class or as those who were firmly in control over there in the Soviet Union.' (In fact, contrary to the Nazi stereotype, Jews were no longer very prominent, with a few exceptions, in the Soviet leadership.)

This comforting prejudice also made the killing of the Soviet political officers, the commissars, easier. 'Our task was absolutely clear to us,' says Walter Traphöner, a soldier in an SS cavalry regiment that fought in the East. 'We knew that Bolshevism was the World-Enemy Number One.... And we were told that their aim was to over-run Germany and France and the whole of Europe down to and including Spain. That's why we had to fight.' In the context of this fight against 'World-Enemy Number One' the commissars were 'particularly dangerous' and 'when we caught any of them, they just had to be killed'. When pressed on how it could be right to execute somebody just because of their political opinions, Traphöner replied: 'We never really asked about the reasons for anything much. I mean they were just blokes who were supporting their system, just like it was with us.... The commissars just had to be killed.... We wanted to prevent the Bolsheviks from conquering the world.'

Back in Moscow, Stalin was coaxed out of his dacha at the end of June after two days, when a delegation from the Politburo 'convinced' him to lead the Soviet Union to victory. (At least one historian believes that Stalin, in retreating to his dacha, was following a ruse of Ivan the Terrible's – feigning collapse to see who supported him and who didn't.) In any event, there was no alternative leader of the Soviet Union. Stalin had helped get them into this disastrous situation – now he would have to help them get out of it.

OPPOSITE A common sight during the German occupation – a body left hanging in a village as a reminder of how the invaders intended to punish the merest infringement.

On 3 July Stalin finally made a radio broadcast to the Soviet people and spoke about the German invasion. 'Comrades, citizens, brothers and sisters, men of our Army and Navy,' he began (the reference to 'brothers and sisters' was significant – it appealed to a nationalist rather than Communist sentiment), 'my words are addressed to you, dear friends! The perfidious military attack begun on 22 June is continuing. In spite of the heroic resistance of the Red Army, and although the enemy's finest divisions and finest Air Force units have already been smashed and have met their doom, Hitler's troops have succeeded in capturing Lithuania, a considerable part of Latvia, the western part of Belorussia and part of western Ukraine. The Fascist aircraft are extending the range of their operation, bombing Murmansk, Orsha, Mogilev, Smolensk, Kiev, Odessa, Sevastopol. Grave danger overhangs our country. How could it happen that our glorious Red Army surrendered a number of our cities and districts to the Fascist armies? Is it really true that the German-Fascist troops are invincible, as the braggart Fascist propagandists are ceaselessly blaring forth? Of course not!'

Stalin went on to defend the Soviet Union's participation in the Non-Aggression Pact ('we secured our country's peace for a year and a half') and to promise military success ('this short-lived military gain for Germany is only an episode'). But there is no disguising the defensiveness of his comments nor the self-justifying thread that runs through them.

One way out for Stalin, of course, would have been to try to make peace with the Germans. There was a precedent for this. In order to extricate the Soviet Union from World War I and to consolidate the Revolution, Lenin had concluded the Treaty of Brest-Litovsk. Under this agreement, which Lenin never intended to be permanent, he had ceded large tracts of territory (nearly 1.4 million square kilometres, including Latvia, Lithuania, Estonia, the Ukraine, Georgia and Armenia) to Germany. Was something like this contemplated – even as an option – in the first weeks of this war? In the rigid Communist version of the history of their 'Great Patriotic War' any peace treaty with the Germans would have been unthinkable treachery. (And any peace negotiations would also, incidentally, have broken the treaty of alliance signed by Britain and the Soviet Union on 12 July, which stated that neither country would 'negotiate nor conclude an armistice or treaty of peace [with Germany] except by mutual agreement'.)

The truth is rather different. Anecdotal rumours that approaches were made through one of Beria's agents to get Ivan Stamenov, the Bulgarian Ambassador in Moscow, to intercede with the Germans have been known in the West for many years. But no document from the Communist period confirmed it – until now. A research team led by Professor Vladimir Naumov, one of the academic consultants for the television series on which this book is based, recently discovered in the Presidential Archive in Moscow a report from Pavel Sudoplatov, one of Beria's most trusted officers. This report was written in 1953 at the time of Beria's arrest, and describes how an approach to the Bulgarian Ambassador took place between 25 and 27 July 1941. Sudoplatov writes: 'Beria instructed me to pose four questions in my discussion with Stamenov. Beria listed these questions looking at his notebook and they amounted to the following:

'1. Why did Germany break its pact of non-invasion and start a war with the USSR?

'2. If Germany were to arrange it, under what conditions would Germany agree to stop the war?

'3. Would the Germans be happy with the handing over of such Soviet lands as the Baltic States, the Ukraine, Bessarabia, Bukovina and the Karelian peninsula?

'4. If not, which territories would Germany want in addition?'

In 1991, shortly before his death, Sudoplatov was interviewed by the KGB about his life as an officer of its predecessor, the NKVD. He briefly mentioned the Stamenov affair, recalling that Beria had been supposed to meet Stamenov personally but Molotov had objected since 'it would be too official' if he went. Sudoplatov also revealed that Stamenov was selected as the go-between not just because as Bulgarian Ambassador he now represented German interests in the Soviet Union, but also because Beria believed that he was sympathetic to the Soviet cause. Beria had done Stamenov favours in the past, including organizing a job in Moscow for his wife, and Sudoplatov goes so far as to describe Stamenov as a Soviet agent.

Pavel Sudoplatov, the intelligence officer whom Beria chose to visit the Aragvi restaurant and make contact with the Bulgarian Ambassador.

On Beria's orders the meeting was to take place at the Georgian Aragvi restaurant in Moscow. Sudoplatov records that his boss added one more condition: 'Beria gave me the strictest warning that I should never tell anyone, anywhere, at any time about this commission of the Soviet government; otherwise myself and my family would be destroyed.'

Sudoplatov dutifully posed the four questions to Stamenov in Beria's private room at the Aragvi restaurant. The Bulgarian Ambassador reacted nonchalantly. 'Stamenov tried to behave as a man convinced of Germany's defeat in the war. He attached little significance to Germany's rapid gains during the first few days of the war. The thrust of what he said boiled down to the USSR's forces, without question, surpassing those of the Germans, and that even if during the initial period the Germans took substantial territory from the USSR and maybe even reached the Volga, in the long run Germany would none the less suffer defeat and would be smashed.' Immediately after the meeting, according to Sudoplatov, he briefed Beria on his conversation with the ambassador; his own involvement in these peace feelers stopped at this point.

What are we to make of this report? It was written in the context of the attack on Beria after Stalin's death. That explains one strange contradiction: at the beginning of the report Sudoplatov writes that he believed Beria was acting with the full consent of the Soviet government, whilst at the end he says he is now convinced (because of what Beria's 'investigators' have just told him) that his former boss acted on his own in 'these actions of betrayal and sabotage'. Obviously, the report has no merit as an attack unless it is asserted that Beria was acting alone, but this is implausible and illogical – what possible reason could Beria have to think that it was worth pursuing an individual attempt to gain peace? Equally, since Beria's career was built upon his closeness and subservience to Stalin, why would he take such a gigantic risk and act in this way without his master's consent, especially since Stalin *was* the Soviet leadership, as head of the government, Defence Commissar, Supreme Commander-in-Chief and Party General Secretary?

Sudoplatov also writes that Beria told him the motive for this approach to Stamenov was to give 'the Soviet government room to manoeuvre and gain time to muster strength'. After the fall of Communism he reiterated that 'the aim of this disinformation was to play for time'. This justification too should be treated with scepticism. For even if this peace approach had been deadly serious, Beria would still have briefed Sudoplatov in this way – it would be the only possible means of denial if news of any negotiations leaked out. 'Of course,' Beria would say, 'this was all part of a massive disinformation campaign....' This also meant that, should the negotiations subsequently be discovered (as they indeed were, and used against Beria at his trial in 1953), there was a chance they might be explained away.

The Russian historian Dimitri Volkogonov, drawing on previously secret sources for his biography of Stalin, unearthed evidence that also contradicts the idea that the Soviet leadership was, by these actions, merely trying to 'gain time to muster strength'. He writes that 'Molotov described the offer of territory in exchange for an end to the fighting as "a possible second Brest-Litovsk Treaty", and said that if Lenin could have the courage to make such a step, we had the same intention now'.

The final significant feature of Sudoplatov's hitherto secret report is the date of the contact with the Bulgarian Ambassador – late July 1941. This means that the following anecdotal story told by a Russian historian who knew Marshal Zhukov becomes of particular importance. In the 1960s Zhukov was out of favour and Professor Viktor Anfilov befriended him. Zhukov told him how he was called to Stalin's dacha in early October 1941, at the lowest point of Soviet fortunes: 'When I was asked in I said, "Good afternoon, Comrade Stalin." Stalin obviously failed to hear me – he was sitting with his back to me. He continued talking to Beria, who

Georgy Zhukov, whose tactical brilliance and personal ruthlessness made him the greatest Soviet commander of the war.

was in his room. And I overheard the following: "...get in touch through your agents with the German intelligence service, find out what Germany is going to want from us if we offer to sign a separate peace treaty".'

Until recently there was dispute about when this approach to the Bulgarian Ambassador had taken place – July or October. Sudoplatov is clear – it was in late July. Yet Zhukov overheard the conversation between Stalin and Beria in October. Therefore what the confirmation of the date of the original approach to the Bulgarian Ambassador in July now leads to is the new and intriguing possibility that, with Stalin's authorization, Beria was ordered to pursue peace feelers in both July and October (and maybe in between as well). And if Zhukov honestly and accurately reported what he heard Stalin saying to Beria, this doesn't sound like 'disinformation' but desperation. It's not surprising, therefore, that after the war the Soviet leadership wanted to pretend that these thoughts were never in their minds – or at least to shove the blame solely on to the shoulders of Beria and Sudoplatov. Just as German generals wanted to rewrite the past once the result of the war was known, so did Stalin and the rest of the Soviet leadership.

During the first months of the invasion, the Germans, of course, weren't about to let

Stalin make even a humiliating peace – not least because, as a result of their victories, they were accumulating Soviet prisoners by the million. 'I witnessed the huge, incredibly enormous numbers of prisoners of war,' says Rüdiger von Reichert, 'which naturally left a deep impression, and helped to get rid of any scepticism one had had when the war started.' The sight of these Soviet prisoners also confirmed to Reichert the accuracy of the Nazi stereotype of the 'sub-human' Slav: 'You saw people who you felt were inferior to you in terms of their level of civilization, their spiritual and mental capabilities – I'm ashamed to say this now, for today we see things entirely differently.'

The fate of these Soviet prisoners of war is one that has not received, in the West, the attention it deserves. Knowledge of the 6 million who died in the Holocaust is, rightly, widespread. But how many in the West know the terrifying statistic that out of a total of 5.7 million Soviet soldiers taken prisoner between June 1941 and February 1945 a staggering 3.3 million died – the majority as a result of disease and starvation? The treatment these POWs received was very different from that experienced by captured British or US servicemen. For the Soviet prisoners there was often no food, no shelter, no camp to speak of at all – just an open field enclosed with barbed wire. The experience of Georgy Semenyak, captured by the Germans near Minsk in July 1941, was typical. Once taken prisoner, he and 80,000 of his comrades were herded into a vast open space, guarded by German soldiers with machine guns. For the first week they

ABOVE AND OPPOSITE
Soviet prisoners of war
photographed by Rüdiger
von Reichert in a camp
in the Ukraine in 1941.
He felt that these
prisoners were 'inferior'
to the Germans.

OVERLEAF A German
soldier stands watch over
one of the gigantic open-
air prison camps
established behind the
front line. More than
3 million Soviet POWs
died in conditions like
these during the war.

were given neither food nor water – they could drink only from a muddy stream at the edge of the camp. At the start of the second week the Germans threw a few boxes of food – mostly salted herring – into the crowd of prisoners and then watched as the Soviet prisoners fought for the contents.

That autumn Semenyak was transferred to an even worse camp in Poland. About 100,000 Soviet prisoners were held in an open space without shelter from the elements. To amuse themselves the German guards would often fire directly into the camp. Lice were everywhere, and as a result there was an epidemic of typhus. A combination of disease, hunger and desperation led to cannibalism amongst the prisoners. During the night bodies were cut open. The buttocks, the liver, the lungs – all were removed, to be fried and then eaten. After beating the odds and surviving all this horror (and without, he says, resorting to cannibalism himself), Semenyak sums up his treatment at the hands of the Germans simply: 'They just never considered us humans.'

After the war some German officers claimed that such huge numbers of prisoners had never been anticipated, so the German Army had lacked the necessary means to deal with them. But at the very least, this is disingenuous. Whilst no direct evidence has surfaced that in the planning stages of the war the death of so many prisoners was specifically ordered, there is more than sufficient circumstantial evidence to conclude that such suffering was an obvious consequence of the way the war was conceived.

During the planning stage of Barbarossa it became clear that the vast distances to the front line and the inadequate Soviet transport system would prevent German troops being adequately supplied from the Reich. By 1941–2 the 'entire German Army' would therefore, as a document of 2 May 1941 from the Wehrmacht's central economic agency states, have to 'be fed at the expense of Russia'. The consequence of this was obvious, as the document records: 'Thereby tens of millions of men will undoubtedly starve to death if we take away all we need from the country.'

Another document from the same agency, dated 23 May that year, goes even further in its prediction of the consequences of the German invasion on the Soviet people's food supply. Entitled 'Political-Economic Guidelines for the Economic Organization East', it states that the goal was to use Russian resources not just for feeding the German Army but also for supplying Nazi-controlled Europe. As a consequence, 30 million Soviet people in the northern part of the region to be occupied were expected to die of starvation.

OPPOSITE Hitler in thoughtful mood. To the left of him are three powerful generals – Wilhelm Keitel, Heinz Guderian and (staring at the camera) Alfred Jodl.

The Wehrmacht leadership must have foreseen that large numbers of Soviet prisoners would be taken – even if they did not anticipate as many as 3 million in the first seven months. But adequate preparations were not taken even for a lower number of captives – hardly surprising given the tone of documents like those quoted above. If, in planning the war, it was possible to assert that perhaps 30 million people would die of starvation as a result of German policy, then why, in parallel, would anyone have been trying actively to save the defeated enemy's soldiers?

That summer, whilst the Soviet prisoners of war died in the German camps, Hitler became concerned about the state of his army's advance. Despite the initial power of the German attack, the Soviet system showed no signs of imminent collapse. And although enormous numbers of prisoners had been taken, the Soviets had been able to call up military reserves – something the Germans had underestimated. In places the Red Army was putting up fierce resistance. Above all there were problems caused by the sheer scale of the German operation. By the middle of July some Panzer units were over 600 kilometres inside Soviet territory and the view voiced before the campaign that such units could, if necessary, 'live off the land' was proving to be a ridiculous fiction. The Soviets had burnt or otherwise destroyed anything that could be of value to the Germans, and supplies from the rear were hampered not only by the distances involved but also by the poor Russian infrastructure (almost all the roads were unmetalled, and what railway track existed was a broader gauge than the German system). In addition, the forward Panzer spearheads had suffered terrible losses. This was only to be expected in Blitzkrieg, where these units bore the brunt of any enemy resistance – Walter Schaefer-Kehnert's spearhead Panzer unit, for example, lost 50 per cent of its personnel within the first eight weeks of the war. But Blitzkrieg operations were not designed to last for month after month.

In July and August 1941 there was conflict at the Wolf's Lair, Hitler's Field Headquarters in East Prussia, between the Führer and his generals. The argument was over how to deal with a new strategic problem. The German front was effectively cut in half by the Pripet Marshes, a remote area all but impenetrable to armoured forces. Whilst Army Group Centre, operating north of the marshes, had made spectacular gains, Army Group South, fighting south of this region, had run into tougher resistance. Hitler's generals still favoured Army Group Centre pushing forward at once to Moscow. Hitler disagreed; not only had he asserted since December 1940 that it was more important to destroy the industrial base of the Soviet Union than to capture its capital, but he was concerned about possible flank attacks on Army Group Centre.

The atmosphere was not helped when Hitler, suffering from dysentery in the early days of August, vacillated about what the German Army should do next. One day Moscow was going to be the priority, then a few days later he insisted that there were other tasks to fulfil first. On 19 August it appeared to Josef Goebbels, the Propaganda Minister, that Hitler might even be doubting the ability of the German Army to crush the Red Army as planned: 'The Führer is very annoyed at himself for letting himself be fooled about the potential of the Bolsheviks by reports from the Soviet Union. His underestimation of the enemy's armoured divisions and Air Force, in particular, has meant an extraordinary amount of trouble for our military operations. He has suffered greatly as a result. It is a serious crisis.' On 21 August Hitler made his decision clear: more important than the capture of Moscow was the encirclement of Leningrad in the north and the destruction of Soviet forces in the south, which would eliminate the threat of a flank attack on Army Group Centre.

Subsequently, this decision has been seen by some as another example of the ignorant corporal crippling the chance of victory created by his generals. But compelling military studies demonstrate that it was Hitler who had the more sound military sense. An advance on Moscow in August by Army Group Centre would have been fraught with risk – not least from flanking attack, since considerable Soviet forces were still concentrated south of the Pripet Marshes in the Ukraine. The Germans might have reached Moscow but then been cut off inside the city, as they were later at Stalingrad.

Hitler's decision to order Guderian's Panzer Group south to Kiev in the Ukraine brought about an astonishing victory – one which restored the Führer's optimism. The Germans took more than 600,000 prisoners at Kiev in the greatest encirclement battle fought in modern times. Whole Soviet armies were caught, some trapped on the eastern bank of the River Dnieper as Kiev fell on 18 September.

Stalin was responsible for this disaster. Dominating the Stavka, the command body that controlled all Soviet forces, and believing in his own genius despite his almost total ignorance of military strategy, he ordered the Red Army to attempt the impossible and hold Kiev. One of the very few who dared stand up to him was Zhukov. He suggested to Stalin that the Red Army should withdraw in the face of the German advance on Kiev, only to be told by Stalin that he was talking 'rubbish'. Zhukov asked to be relieved at once of his post as Chief of the General Staff – a proposal that Stalin instantly accepted.

Nikolay Ponomariev, Stalin's personal telegraphist, witnessed the Soviet leader's response to the frantic calls from the Red Army commanders in Kiev. 'They were saying that they were not strong enough to maintain control over Kiev,' he says. 'They asked to be allowed to move the troops away, but Stalin insisted on the opposite – "Hold out as long as you can."' Stalin's intransigence cost the Soviet Army dear – the paucity of his strategic thinking is no better illustrated than by this catastrophe. Stalin's idea of defence at this time was as simple as Hitler's was later to become – hold your ground and fight to the last.

German soldiers were elated. 'We succeeded, didn't we!' says Hubert Menzel, who fought as a German tank officer at Kiev. 'We did wage encirclement battles across distances which we'd been simply incapable of imagining before.' Hitler too was euphoric. This was, he believed, the turning point of the war.

A German soldier fights house-to-house during the capture of the Ukrainian capital, Kiev, in 1941.

With the threat from the flanks now clear, Hitler accepted that the German Army should push on towards Moscow, with the Soviet capital the target of the German Operation Typhoon.

On the Soviet side, in the wake of the dramatic loss of Kiev, there was bewilderment and fear. 'We simply kept wondering why our Army was surrendering one town after another,' says Viktor Strazdovski, who was 18 years old in 1941. 'It was a real tragedy. It's difficult to express by words how we lived through that.' That autumn Strazdovski joined the Red Army and was shocked to see the equipment he was expected to use to defend his country. 'The 60-millimetre guns that we were given were trophies left from World War I – they didn't have modern sighting devices. And we only had one rifle between five soldiers.'

Strazdovski, badly equipped and poorly trained, was about to take part in the Battle of Vyazma – around the town that was the last great obstacle in the way of the German advance on Moscow. At the beginning of October 1941 the 3rd and 4th Panzer Groups linked to form the Vyazma pocket. Five Soviet armies were trapped. 'We were face to face with the Germans,' says Strazdovski, 'and we had to use these primitive weapons in real combat. We didn't feel confident enough.... When I was sent to the place where the Germans broke our defence line, you can imagine how we felt – we felt we were doomed. There were four of us, with two rifles between us, and we didn't know in which direction we would run into the Germans. The woods around us were ablaze. On the one hand we couldn't disobey our order, but on the other hand we felt doomed.'

Soviet soldiers tried frantically to break through and escape the German encirclement. 'I saw one of these attacks coming early in the morning,' says Walter Schaefer-Kehnert, an officer in the 11th Panzer Division. 'We were sitting on top of the hills, there was a fog going down to the river valley, and when the fog came up it was like a herd of vehicles and men coming up by the thousand and it made your blood freeze...and then the Russians came into the ground where there was a swampy area, and then all the vehicles at once sunk in the mud, and then the people came on to us like a herd of sheep.' Schaefer-Kehnert shouted to his men, 'Let them come, let them get nearer, let them come on!' until they were close enough for the German 2-centimetre anti-aircraft flak cannon and machine guns to mow them down.

The next day Schaefer-Kehnert looked out over the battlefield at the thousands of Soviet dead and dying lying in front of him: 'And there were some Russian girls – I will never forget them – in trousers and dressed like soldiers, and they got in a cart, with

a horse, and had a barrel of water and then went around giving water to the dying Russian soldiers lying on that field.... They were lying there by the thousand like the battlefield of old history.'

Wolfgang Horn was in another Panzer division at Vyazma facing a different section of the encircled Soviet armies. As he looked across at the Red Army through special field glasses, he saw an 'incredible' sight. Only the front row of Soviet soldiers rushing towards the Germans had rifles – the row behind was unarmed. 'As the first row was mowed down,' says Horn, 'they [the second row] bent down and took the guns of those who were dead – they were destined to attack without weapons...something that was totally unfamiliar to us.'

That night, as more Soviet troops tried to find a way past the Germans, Horn's unit spotted several trucks full of Red Army soldiers coming towards them. The Soviet soldiers opened fire. But standing close together in the trucks they made a 'beautiful target' for Horn and his comrades, who lobbed hand grenades at them. Horn himself sustained a minor wound, which so angered him that he fought back even more fiercely at the enemy soldiers trapped around their trucks. 'Then the Russians were so cowardly,' says Horn, 'that some of the crew of these trucks cowered behind the vehicle.' As the Soviet soldiers lay huddled together, their hands and arms covering their heads, Horn shouted, 'Hands up!' in Russian at them, and then, when they didn't immediately respond, he and his comrades opened fire and killed them all. 'When they don't surrender,' he says, 'we shoot them. It was natural for us to do.... They are cowards – they didn't deserve any better, anyhow.'

Even if Horn had accepted the surrender of these Soviet soldiers that night, they still might not have been saved because the lieutenant commanding his unit decided to order the murder of many of the Soviet prisoners taken. Horn felt this behaviour not just 'unchivalrous' but 'stupid' because 'Russians hiding in the forest might have seen the prisoners being shot and so they might fight better the next time'.

Viktor Strazdovski sums up the battle succinctly: 'What happened there is like a mincing machine, when people are sent to a sure death, unarmed to fight a well-trained army.' Walter Schaefer-Kehnert came to another conclusion: 'A life wasn't worth much for the Russians. Their deaths were not taken as seriously as with us...we were of the belief that there shouldn't be much left of the Red Army now.'

October 1941 marked the high point of Operation Barbarossa. Army Group

OPPOSITE Red Army volunteer Viktor Strazdovski poses in front of a picture of Stalin. He was soon to experience first hand the destruction of Soviet forces at the encirclement of Vyazma.

OVERLEAF Leningrad during the 900-day German siege of the city, from July 1941 to January 1944. Hitler had stated that Leningrad must 'vanish from the earth' and, not wishing to risk the lives of his soldiers in street fighting (in contrast to Stalingrad), ordered Army Group North to blockade the city into submission. A combination of hunger, cold, illness and the German bombardment claimed the lives of around a million people.

Centre's defeat of the Red Army at Vyazma and the nearby Battle of Bryansk had eliminated the last serious obstacle on the road to Moscow. In the Ukraine, after the capture of Kiev, Army Group South had consolidated its position and the bounty of the Soviet Union's 'breadbasket' lay open to be plundered for the Reich. Outside Leningrad Army Group North had succeeded in cutting off the city and was attempting to starve out the inhabitants. It was the beginning of a 900-day siege of appalling suffering – in the winter of 1941–2 half a million people would die of starvation. All of this German military success led Hitler to declare at the Berlin Sportpalast that the Red Army 'would never rise again'. Jodl remarked: 'We have finally and without any exaggeration won the war!' And

Nikolay Ponomariev, a communications officer in the General Staff Headquarters before the war, who became Stalin's personal telegraphist in 1941.

Otto Dietrich, the Führer's own Press Chief, stated: 'For all military purposes Soviet Russia is done with.'

At Vyazma (combined with the Battle of Bryansk) the Germans took another 660,000 prisoners. The news from the front line filled Muscovites with despair – just 90,000 Soviet troops now defended the capital. In this despondent atmosphere Nikolay Ponomariev, Stalin's telegraphist, was ordered to make contact with Zhukov, now back in favour as Commander of the Western Front, so that the Soviet leader could seek his advice. 'I knew that the situation was really bad,' says Ponomariev. 'Life in Moscow had stopped, the Metro had stopped running. Stalin came up to me, said, "Hello", as if nothing was happening, and asked,

"What are we going to do? The Germans are pushing through to Moscow." I didn't expect such a question. I said, "We can't let the Germans into Moscow, they have to be beaten." "I think so too," he said. "Now let's ask Comrade Zhukov what is his opinion on the subject."'

Stalin listened for more than an hour and a half as Zhukov outlined what he needed for the defence of Moscow – tanks, artillery and, most importantly of all, rockets. 'It was a really difficult conversation,' says Ponomariev. 'I learnt from that how short of supplies and undermanned our army was.' Stalin told Zhukov that at least some of the supplies he needed were already on their way. Then, witnessed by Ponomariev, he asked Zhukov a question. '"Tell me, Georgy Konstantinovich, as a Communist to a Communist, are we going to hold Moscow or not?" Zhukov paused and then replied, "Comrade Stalin, if I get even part of the help that I asked for, we will hold Moscow."'

That was not the end of dramatic events on 16 October 1941, as ten minutes after the phone call to Zhukov one of Stalin's senior aides told Ponomariev to pack all his equipment and get ready to leave. 'Half an hour later,' says Ponomariev, 'I was visited by one of Stalin's security guards, and he asked me if I was ready to go. "Where are we going?" I asked. And he said, "You'll see when you go. Get ready and come with me." There was a car waiting outside. We were driven away. Moscow was completely dark. The weather was wet. I saw we were heading for the railway station. I saw the armoured train and Stalin's guards walking to and fro on the platform. It became clear to me that I would have to wait for Stalin and go into evacuation with him.'

As Ponomariev sat on Stalin's train, other Muscovites came to the conclusion that they too should prepare to leave. Maya Berzina, a 31-year-old mother, was one of those who decided to flee. 'We wondered what would happen if the government left,' she says. 'It must mean that Moscow would be surrendered. My husband was Jewish, I was half-Jewish and it meant we were doomed. My husband ran to the railway station and he was told that there would be no trains...he was advised to leave on foot. We had a three-year-old son and what could we do with him? He was too heavy to carry and too weak to walk. We realized there was also Moscow port, the southern port, and my husband went there and learnt there would be some ships. On that day of panic I saw how people began to show initiative – which was a long-forgotten thing. We're used to directives. It turned out that the chief of the port began to sell tickets for a ship that was already mothballed for the winter and somehow we managed to get on it.'

Maya Berzina was certain, on that day in mid-October, that the Germans would take Moscow: 'We heard there were people who put up posters that said "Welcome". There was panic. We were told by the conductor on the tram that she had seen Germans on another tram – I don't know if it was true.... Directors of shops opened their shops and were saying to people, "Take what you want. We don't want the Germans to get these things."'

In this atmosphere of panic even Stalin himself considered deserting the capital. A secret document only just declassified, number 34 of the State Defence Committee, dated 15 October 1941, reveals just how serious Stalin believed the situation had become. It states that the State Defence Committee had resolved 'To evacuate the Presidium of the Supreme Soviet and the top levels of Government.... (Comrade Stalin will leave tomorrow or later, depending on the situation).... In the event of enemy forces arriving at the gates of Moscow, the NKVD – Comrade Beria and Comrade Shcherbakov – are ordered to blow up business premises, warehouses and institutions which cannot be evacuated, and all Underground railway electrical equipment.'

This was perhaps the key moment of the whole war. For if Stalin had climbed on board his train and fled, Soviet resistance might have weakened decisively. Many believe that, even without Stalin, a combination of the oncoming winter weather and the problems of fighting inside Moscow, street to street, would have broken the Germans. But what that scenario underestimates is the psychological effect of Stalin's presence on the population of Moscow. Many of those Russians we talked to emphasized the importance they placed on their leader's continued presence in Moscow. In propaganda terms Stalin *was* the Soviet Union. If he was a coward, why couldn't everyone be a coward? If he ran, why couldn't they?

Vladimir Ogryzko (front row, second left) with his NKVD unit. They brutally suppressed the panic in Moscow in October 1941.

Perhaps, even if Stalin had deserted the capital, the Germans would have been surrounded and trapped inside Moscow – that's almost certainly what would have happened if Army Group Centre had moved on the Soviet capital in August whilst the threat from the flanks remained. But by October, with that danger eliminated, why couldn't Moscow have become another Kiev or Minsk – cities that the Germans now held securely? Stalin's apparent cowardice and his inability to prevent the growing panic in the capital would have severely damaged his authority. And once the Soviet leadership lost Moscow, the centre of the Soviet communications and transport network, what terms of peace might they have been prepared to negotiate?

In the event, Stalin decided to stay in Moscow – but only after vacillating about what he should do. On 15 October, according to Politburo member Anastas Mikoyan, Stalin announced to them that he intended to leave Moscow 'tomorrow morning'. But by the night of the 19th Stalin had resolved to stay. V. S. Pronin, President of the Moscow Soviet, was present at that decisive meeting. This is his account of what happened – a notable first-hand description of how Stalin conducted business: 'When we assembled in the room leading to Stalin's office Beria set about persuading everyone that we should abandon Moscow. He argued that we should give up Moscow and set up a defensive line on the Volga. Malenkov supported him, Molotov mumbled his disagreement. In fact, I particularly remember Beria's words: "But how are we going to defend Moscow? We have absolutely nothing at all. We have been overwhelmed and we are being shot down like partridges." Then all of us went into Stalin's office. Stalin came in as usual with his pipe. When we had settled down, Stalin asked: "Are we going to defend Moscow?" Everyone was silent. He waited a moment and then repeated his question. Again no reply. "Very well [said Stalin], we will ask individually." Molotov replied first: "We will defend [Moscow]." All, including Beria, answered the same: "We will defend [Moscow]."'

So Stalin decided to stay in Moscow, which he insisted must be held by the harshest measures necessary. In order to counter the panic, he instituted a 'state of siege' in the capital from 20 October. A curfew was imposed from midnight to 5 a.m. and the task of enforcing law and order was entrusted to the NKVD.

Vladimir Ogryzko commanded one of the NKVD units which tried to restore order in Moscow that October. 'Panic was spread by diversionary groups and spies who had broken through Moscow's defences,' he says. 'There were robberies – everything you can imagine happened – because as usual the people lost their heads...the ill-educated ones. The scum of the earth did show its face. It seeped through.'

Men like Ogryzko interpreted Stalin's order as giving them total power. 'It isn't peacetime,' he says. 'You're not going to say, "Stop or I'll shoot!" a thousand times before you shoot, nor are you going to shoot in the air. Of course not. You shoot them on the spot. It was a tough command. Anybody who resisted and didn't obey orders on demand – especially if they moved away or opened their mouths – was eliminated on the spot without further ado. And that was considered a truly heroic act – you were killing the enemy.'

The streets were jammed with fleeing Muscovites, towards whom Ogryzko had a similarly uncompromising attitude. 'They were running away,' he says, 'they were marauders, bastards who thought they'd stay alive at the end of the day.' He overturned their cars into the roadside ditches and 'If the driver was crushed, well, even better...that wasn't my responsibility.'

A combination of Stalin's decision to stay in Moscow and the imposition of this brutal 'state of siege' did indeed restore order. 'These severe measures, these beautiful measures,' says Vladimir Ogryzko, 'are the essence and content of war. You cannot say that they go against human rights – they are neither cruel nor mad. It was right to execute the people who didn't understand their position at a time which had become more cruel for their country.... Had there not been such a tough order, there would have been total panic. Anything could have happened. Literally. It was a very wise, resolute and correct decision taken by the Defence Council and Stalin.'

Outside the city the Germans, as the winter weather began, contemplated the final attack. They had travelled further and faster, and taken more enemy prisoners, than any invading army in history. The only problem was that, according to their original plan, by now they should already have won the war.

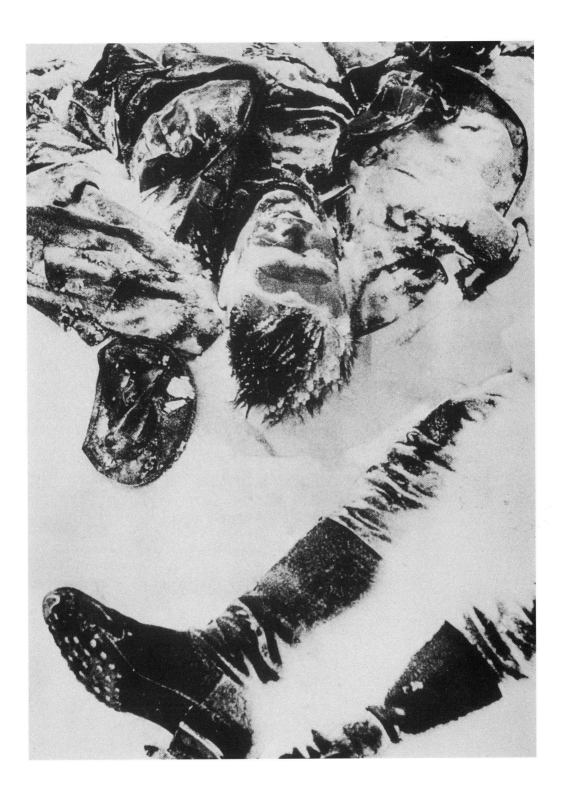

CHAPTER 2

A DIFFERENT KIND OF WAR

More civilians died in this war than any other in history. Around 13 million Soviet civilians alone lost their lives under German occupation (more than twice the entire population of Scotland). Set against the background of the Battle of Moscow and then the Nazi occupation of Soviet territory in 1942 and 1943, this chapter therefore confronts one of the most important questions of the conflict: why did this, of all wars, result in such a human catastrophe?

A key reason, of course, was the character of the respective leaders. Both Hitler and Stalin shared a disregard for the lives of those they ruled. Humanity had no place in their attitude to war. When one acted brutally, the other would respond – with more brutality. Nowhere was that uncompromising attitude to human life made more clear than during the struggle for the Soviet capital.

In mid-October 1941 it looked as if Moscow was about to fall into German hands. But then Stalin decided to stay in the city; NKVD troops quelled the panic and the winter rains began, causing a three-week delay to the German advance as the roads became impassable. Whilst the Germans waited, Zhukov set about enforcing discipline at the front and nine Soviet reserve armies were gathered east of the Volga, bolstered by the arrival of fresh troops from Siberia.

Operation Typhoon, the German advance on Moscow, began again on 15 November, and on the solid, frozen ground made good progress. By the beginning of December a few forward units were about 20 kilometres from the centre of the city – it was as near as the Germans were ever to get. Walter Schaefer-Kehnert's Panzer unit was one of those that came closest, on 4 December. As he studied his maps and examined the position of his artillery

OPPOSITE During the German occupation of Kharkov in the eastern Ukraine, thousands of people, particularly women and children, starved to death.

batteries, he realized an extraordinary truth: 'I measured this distance to the Kremlin and said, "Well, if we had a long-range cannon, we could shoot at the Kremlin."' Through the regimental commander they obtained a 10.5-centimetre gun and opened fire. 'With a 10-centimetre gun you won't do much harm,' he says. 'We thought only of the morale consequences on the citizens of Moscow – shooting to the town and the Kremlin!'

The ineffectual shelling of the Kremlin symbolized the German position – they had come so far and yet still had not accomplished the goal they had set themselves. The next day, 5 December, Schaefer-Kehnert's unit felt the weight of the Soviet counter-attack. As the Germans tried to defend themselves, they were hampered by the sudden, intense cold. 'When the temperature dropped to below minus 30 degrees Celsius our machine guns were not firing any more,' says Schaefer-Kehnert. 'Our machine guns were precision instruments but when the oil got thick they didn't shoot properly any more – this really makes you afraid.' All around him, he saw the devastating effect of the Germans' lack of winter clothing. According to the original Barbarossa plan, two-thirds of the German Army should have been withdrawn by now since the war would already have been won, so proper preparations had never been made for winter warfare. 'We had huge losses from frozen toes and fingers during the night,' says Schaefer-Kehnert. 'And when the infantry had to sleep in the open, you tried to make a hole in the snow. Then there was an order that a guard had to go round every two hours and look because you would freeze to death and you would not realize it was happening. Particularly if we had been fighting during the day and sweating and then we cooled off at night – that was when the greatest danger was of freezing to death. It's a very nice death but you don't want to have it!'

Rüdiger von Reichert's unit suffered when they could no longer move their heavy artillery. The guns were pulled by brewery horses, 'pampered creatures used to an abundance of food and warm stables, and these poor animals now suddenly found themselves drawing heavy pieces of artillery which they had to draw first through quicksand, then mud and then snow. And almost all of them died of heart disease.'

OPPOSITE German soldiers wearing improvised raffia-like covers on their boots. The continuation of the war into the Russian winter caught them ill-prepared.

'The German Army near Moscow was a very miserable sight,' says Fyodor Sverdlov, a company commander in the Soviet 19th Rifle Brigade. 'I remember very well the Germans in July 1941. They were confident, strong, tall guys. They marched ahead with their sleeves rolled up and carrying their machine guns.

But later on they became miserable, crooked, snotty guys wrapped in woollen kerchiefs stolen from old women in villages.... Of course, they were still firing and defending themselves, but they weren't the Germans we knew earlier in 1941.'

Whilst the Soviet counter-attack continued, on 7 December Hitler received what he took to be good news – the Japanese had bombed Pearl Harbor. He believed this meant that the United States, with its hands tied by a wide-ranging Pacific War, would no longer be able to devote resources to helping Britain and consequently the Soviet Union. Only days earlier Hitler had been briefed by Fritz Todt, Reich Minister for Armaments and Munitions, that if the USA entered the conflict, the war would be lost for Germany. But Hitler still chose to see American involvement via Japan as a positive sign. On 11 December Germany formally declared war on the United States. To Hitler this was doing little more than recognizing the inevitable; ever since the Americans had begun their package of war aid to the British, he had foreseen an eventual confrontation with the USA unless Britain could be removed from the conflict first. That, after all, had been one of the key reasons behind Operation Barbarossa – Hitler had wanted to eliminate the threat from the East before an American-backed front opened in Europe. Unfortunately for Hitler, not only had the Red Army not been destroyed in 1941 as planned, but the opening of hostilities between Japan and the USA and the subsequent Japanese advance south to Singapore meant that Stalin could now release more Soviet troops from his Western border, confident that he would not fall victim to an attack from the Japanese, Germany's Axis ally. With its military machine fully occupied on land fighting the British, and in the Pacific confronting the mighty American fleet, it was not in Japan's interests to provoke any conflict with the Soviet Union.

By the middle of December the situation of the German troops outside Moscow had become desperate. Halder called their predicament 'the greatest crisis in two world wars' and summed up a report from the Quartermaster General as saying 'we have reached the end of our human and material forces'.

On 16 December Hitler ordered the German forces to stand firm, believing that any retreat might turn into a rout. He issued a directive to Army Group Centre calling for the 'fanatical will to defend the ground on which the troops are standing' to be 'injected' into the troops. If a staged withdrawal was ever necessary, then 'every place of inhabitation must be burnt down and destroyed without consideration for the population'.

The Panzer commander, Heinz Guderian, objected fiercely to Hitler's order. He argued that to insist the Army stood where it was would result in the senseless death of German soldiers. They must retreat. Hitler seemed bemused by these objections. 'Do you think Frederick the Great's Grenadiers enjoyed dying for their country either?' he asked. Revealingly, he then criticized Guderian. 'You stand too close to events,' Hitler remarked. 'You ought to disengage yourself more.'

Germans surrender to the Red Army in the winter of 1941–2.

Hitler's obvious contempt for those, like Guderian, who expressed any pity for human suffering was another key reason why the war became so brutal. In a crisis he believed the stronger 'will' would prevail – and 'will' became a synonym for cruelty. He always felt his generals had a dangerous tendency towards pity – indeed, at a meeting with his military commanders in August 1939, just days before the invasion of Poland, he had told them to remember, 'It is not machines that fight each other but men,' and that they must 'Close [their] hearts to pity. Act brutally.' Now, his generals were failing him. On 22 December Guderian was relieved of his command. A few days earlier, on the 19th, Field Marshal von Brauchitsch had retired because of ill health. He received none of the

traditional decorations or honours due on retirement. Instead he was vilified. Here – to committed Nazis – was another example of a German general who just hadn't demonstrated the strength of 'will' the Führer had a right to demand. Goebbels recorded in his diary the following March that Hitler called Brauchitsch 'a vain, cowardly wretch who could not even appraise the situation, much less master it'. Goebbels also recorded his own view that 'The senior officers who have risen from the General Staff are incapable of withstanding severe strain and major tests of character.' The pure Nazi view is here clearly expressed – deficient equipment and inadequate supplies were not symptomatic of disastrous planning but were, in fact, 'major tests of character'.

As Wolfgang Horn and the rest of his unit discovered that winter, even getting frostbite would be to fail this 'major test of character': 'We had to warn each other if a nose was getting white. "Rub your nose otherwise you will be punished!" You see, those who had something frozen were punished for abandoning the Fatherland to some degree – sabotaging the war effort by letting something freeze.'

This same ruthless desire to enforce the harshest discipline on those who thought of retreat was evident on the Soviet side as well. As an NKVD officer, Vladimir Ogryzko fought alongside rearguard divisions behind the troops in the Battle of Moscow. Their job was simple. If Soviet troops ran past them in retreat, they killed them. 'The station I was protecting had the right to kill anyone who approached it,' says Ogryzko. 'They're given a chance, when you say, "Stop or I'll shoot!" And if they don't stop, then they're shot.... There are a certain number of rules in life, especially in the army and even more so in war. There can't be demagogues. They are traitors, simply traitors. It should be considered as part of people's education – a traitor should get his come-uppance.' Ogryzko is still proud of his work: 'It was a very good decision to take and it shouldn't be judged. They used fear to crush fear. If it was right or wrong, so what? It was a time of war and there had to be certainty.'

Just as Hitler's personality helped shape the nature of the German defence outside Moscow, so Stalin's helped shape the Red Army's attack: 'I have to say that the cruelty and determination and will of Stalin were communicated to the commanders of the front and also reached us, the junior commanders,' says Fyodor Sverdlov, commander of an infantry company at the Battle of Moscow. 'Stalin was cruel, but even now I continue to think this cruelty was justified. There couldn't be any mercy, any pity.'

OPPOSITE Fyodor Sverdlov, an infantry officer during the Battle of Moscow. He admits that Soviet forces were always drunk at 'decisive' moments of the war, and looks 'happy' enough here.

During a frank interview, Sverdlov admitted that in pursuit of Stalin's 'cruel' policy he personally shot one of his own men. 'It happened once during a successful attack. There was one soldier, I don't know what his name was, but because of his cowardice and because the combat was very severe he broke down, and he began to run, and I killed him without thinking twice. And that was a good lesson to all the rest.'

Sverdlov also revealed another element that contributed to the brutality of the conflict – he, and the men he commanded, often fought under the influence of alcohol: 'There's a Russian saying that a drunken man can cross the sea. Whenever a man gets drowned in the Moskva River, he would always be a drunk. A drunk thinks that everything is easy,

and this makes it clear why Russian soldiers were given vodka.' Every one of his soldiers was issued with 100 grams of vodka a day from the Ministry of Defence – this was known as the 'Minister's 100'. But this wasn't all they drank. 'You know that Russians are fond of drinking,' he says, 'but it was a must during the war. Of course, it was seldom that we drank 100 grams only because as we bore heavy losses every day that amount of vodka was meant to cover a bigger number of people than there actually were. I usually drank 200 grams of vodka at breakfast, 100 grams of vodka at

German troops enter Bessarabia in the south-west Soviet Union in July 1941. The jubilant welcome was similar to that which had greeted the Germans in Austria in 1938. But this was to be a very different occupation.

lunch, and if there was no combat in the evening, I would drink another 200 gram glass sharing dinner with a company of friends.'

Fyodor Sverdlov doesn't feel that being drunk hampered the fighting ability of the Soviet soldier – quite the contrary: 'When a person gets drunk, he feels more determined, more courageous. He doesn't think about being killed in a minute. He marches on, trying to kill the enemy. Being quite frank, I have to say that in the course of the whole war both Germans and Russians were always drunk at decisive moments because a human mind cannot otherwise bear the horrors of the modern war. I don't know if the British and the Americans drank when they were landing in Normandy, but I bet they drank whisky.'

By the end of January 1942 the crisis was over for the Germans. The front had stabilized. Hitler believed this accomplishment had been his alone – after all, had he not been the one who had issued the stand-fast order? And, his conceit knowing no bounds, he had by now replaced Brauchitsch as Commander-in-Chief of the German Army with the only man he felt certain had the strength of will to do the job properly – himself. But in reality Stalin and his generals were not yet in a position, in either their tactical thinking or the resources at their disposal, to impose a decisive defeat on the German Army. The eventual outcome of the war was far from certain and, in the meantime, the Nazis had a new empire to rule.

The way the Germans administered their conquered territories in the East (particularly the biggest of them all, the Ukraine) was to play another decisive part in the escalation of the brutality of this war. Ironically, given what was to happen, at the start of Operation Barbarossa many German soldiers thought the indigenous population of the East could be their allies, not their enemies. 'During the first few months of the war we were welcomed as liberators,' says Peter von der Groeben, who was a senior officer with the 86th Infantry Division. 'Sometimes they would bring you salt and bread [the traditional symbols of welcome and hospitality] because the peasants considered this their liberation from Bolshevism.' For Rüdiger von Reichert, an artillery officer with the 4th Army, the experience was the same: 'I experienced it again and again in these first months, that people would bring you something from their garden – we were very hungry for fresh vegetables. Not everybody was delighted, but many of them welcomed us warmly as their liberators.'

Many of the German soldiers, even those like Carlheinz Behnke who fought in an SS Panzer division, thought that this might turn into a 'conventional' occupation: 'We assumed that once the Ukraine had been occupied it would become an independent state and the soldiers would probably fight on our side against the rest of the Bolshevists. It might have been naive, but that was the general trend and mood amongst us young soldiers.'

The reason for the warm welcome the German soldiers received as they marched into the Ukraine is not hard to find. The Ukrainians had suffered hugely under rule from Moscow. The famine of the early 1930s – created by Communist policies – had resulted in an estimated 7 million deaths. And just before they retreated in the face of the German advance, the NKVD had murdered thousands of Ukrainian political prisoners. 'We dreamt about the new Ukrainian state,' says Aleksey Bris, who lived in the west of the Ukraine. 'Any war against the Soviet Union was perceived by us as a good war.'

As an 18-year-old student with a gift for languages, Bris started to work for the local German administration as an interpreter. As he sees it, this was not collaboration: 'I mean, every man is dreaming to have something better. Nobody would like to be a sweeper on the street.' For him, and for many other Ukrainians, the Germans appeared at first as just another in a long line of conquerors. And 'under all authorities, regardless of their character, their particular system was accepted as "normal". For example, if the Chinese had come, we would also have thought of them as "normal"...I would have to work for them somehow because I need to eat, I need to live, I need to work, and that's why we didn't have this kind of definition as "collaboration" as you have it in the West.' As Bris saw it, the Ukrainians had 'no other choice' but to work with the Germans.

Aleksey Bris's decision to assist the Germans was based on the judgement that the Nazis were 'like any other conqueror'. But they weren't. Hitler did not believe in a policy of cooperation with the indigenous population of the Eastern territories – in the way the British had ruled India or, indeed, the way the Romans had governed their empire. Whilst the conquered people in the West of the Nazi Empire, like the French or Dutch, could generally be treated less brutally because they were for the most part 'civilized', Hitler believed that since the people of the Soviet Union were 'inferior', they did not deserve the resources that nature had given them. 'It's inconceivable,' he said, 'that a higher people [i.e. the Germans] should painfully exist on a soil too narrow for it, whilst amorphous masses, which contribute nothing to civilization, occupy infinite tracts of a soil that is one of the richest in the world.' Hitler preached that the Germans should be guided by only one natural law in this occupation – the stronger person must do whatever he liked. As he put it: 'The earth continues to go round, whether it's the man who kills the tiger or the tiger who eats the man. The stronger asserts his will, it's the law of nature.'

ABOVE Alfred Rosenberg, Minister of the Eastern Territories (second left), and Erich Koch, Reichskommissar for the Ukraine (second right): they loathed each other.

OPPOSITE Erich Koch, Reichskommissar for the Ukraine, was also Gauleiter of East Prussia. He joined the Nazi Party in 1922 and was one of Hitler's oldest comrades.

Such a philosophy freed Hitler to dream of a form of conquest that would crush the inhabitants of the occupied Eastern territories for ever; incredibly, he saw his mission to make them less civilized than even he thought they already were. Their level of education was to be, as he described it, 'just enough to understand our highway signs so that they won't get themselves run over by our vehicles'. For all his admiration for the British achievement in India, Hitler looked across the Atlantic to the violent colonization of the American West for a practical lesson in how to deal with the population of the German-occupied territories: 'There's only one duty: to Germanize this country by the immigration of Germans, and to look upon the natives as Redskins.'

These extracts, from Hitler's private dinner-table monologues, carry the stamp of the authentic Führer. But he was not always so forthright, as Alfred Rosenberg, newly appointed Minister of the Eastern Territories, was to discover. Rosenberg met Hitler on 16 July 1941 at the Führer's headquarters in East Prussia, the Wolf's Lair, and voiced his view that the nationalist sentiments of the Ukrainians should be encouraged. Hitler did not object. At a later conference Hitler even hinted that the Ukraine might one day be considered independent within the German Empire. But these were simply words to keep the loyal but misguided Rosenberg happy. On 19 September Hitler revealed his true feelings to a more ideologically sympathetic Nazi. Notes survive of a meeting between Hitler and Erich Koch, the Nazi

Gauleiter of East Prussia and recently appointed Reich Commissioner for the Ukraine. 'Both the Führer and the Reichskommissar [Koch] reject an independent Ukraine.... Besides, hardly anything will be left standing in Kiev [the capital]. The Führer's inclination to destroy Russia's large cities as a prerequisite for the permanence of our power in Russia will be further consolidated by the Reichskommissar's smashing of Ukrainian industry, in order to drive the proletariat back to the land.'

What pleasure it must have given Hitler, in a meeting with a Nazi hard-liner like Koch, to state that it was his 'inclination to destroy Russia's large cities'. Here he could be honest. With Rosenberg, technically Koch's superior in the Nazi hierarchy, for long periods he was more opaque. Such behaviour seems curious at first, since it was Hitler himself who appointed Rosenberg. But Hitler's behaviour is explicable, consistent as it is with the methods he generally used to control and manipulate the Nazi state.

In the first place, Nazi hierarchies were not what they seemed. Koch had a very large degree of autonomy in how he decided to run the Ukraine and he was able to report directly to Hitler, should he wish it, through the automatic access guaranteed by his other position as Gauleiter of East Prussia, so Rosenberg could be bypassed whenever necessary. Second, Hitler was always loyal to those, like Rosenberg, who had stuck by him in the times of 'struggle' before the Nazis came to power – and here was a grand-sounding job as a reward for his loyalty. Third, the appointment of Rosenberg allowed Hitler to play off Koch against him if he wanted to. In-fighting amongst leading Nazis preserved the Führer's role as the final arbiter within the system. Finally, Hitler disliked issuing written orders to the likes of Rosenberg and Koch, so the presence of this conflict between them allowed him 'deniability' if anything went catastrophically wrong. As Hitler acknowledged when he spoke to the commanding generals of the German Army Groups in the summer of 1942, he was prepared to say whatever he felt any situation demanded: 'Were it not for the psychological effect, I would go as far as I could; I would say, "Let's set up a fully independent Ukraine." I would say it without blinking and then not do it anyway. That I could do as a politician, but (since I must say it publicly) I can't tell every [German] soldier just as publicly: "It isn't true; what I've just said is only tactics."'

Inevitably, there was a series of disruptive rows between Rosenberg and Koch about how the Ukraine should be run. Whilst Rosenberg toyed with the idea of treating the Ukraine in a more conventional colonial way, Koch's attitude is best expressed in his statement to the Nazis on Kiev city administration that 'we are a master race that must remember, the lowliest German worker is racially and biologically a thousand times more valuable than the population here'. Whilst Rosenberg dreamt one day of a university in Kiev, Koch closed the schools saying, 'Ukrainian children need no schools. What they have to learn will be taught them by their German masters.'

'You would not believe the kind of confusion there was,' says Dr Wilhelm Ter-Nedden, who worked in Rosenberg's ministry in Berlin. 'The administration melted away.' Even though Rosenberg was technically his superior, Koch treated him with open contempt. Ter-Nedden attended meetings between the two men and was shocked at what he saw: 'On these occasions I witnessed Koch tearing Rosenberg off a strip, in such a manner that I would have thrown him out! And Rosenberg put up with it.' At one lunch Koch ignored Rosenberg completely, only talking to the person next to him, until finally he leaned across the table and said loudly, 'Is this as boring for you, Rosenberg, as it is for me?' To Ter-Nedden this was all symptomatic of the same warped political system that had previously allowed Hermann Göring to control the economic destiny of Germany via the Four-Year Plan: 'When Göring arrived we all had to line up to meet him – and Göring said, roughly, "Of course, I know nothing about economics, but I have an unbridled will!"'

Koch's own 'unbridled will' was creating a very different Ukraine from the one Aleksey Bris had anticipated: 'Little by little, between Germans and Ukrainians there was a feeling of separation – an edge.' To Bris this was summed up one day by a conversation he had with Ernst Erich Haerter, the German commissar of Horokhiv, his local town. Bris said that one day he would like to continue his studies and become a doctor. The German commissar replied, echoing Koch: 'We don't need you Ukrainians as doctors or engineers, we need you as people to tend the cows.' As Bris now saw it, the Germans regarded themselves as 'gods on the earth'.

However, Nazi policy towards these occupied territories was never straightforward, and not just because of the inherent tension between functionaries like Rosenberg and Koch. Sometimes it was impossible for Nazi administrators accurately to second-guess just what the Führer's policy would be on any particular issue, as the saga of the availability of contraceptives to the Ukrainians amply demonstrates.

In July 1942 Hitler moved from East Prussia to new field headquarters near the town of Vinnitsa in the Ukraine, and stayed there until October of that year. This location allowed his faithful lieutenant, Martin Bormann, to observe the local population in the surrounding villages. He was outraged at what he saw; the Ukrainian children did not look like sub-humans at all. On the contrary, many were blond and blue-eyed. Seeking an explanation of this phenomenon in Nazi evolutionary theory, he concluded that these impressive children were the product of their grim living conditions – as a consequence of the poor housing and sanitation only the strongest children had survived. It was not in the interests of the Reich, as Bormann saw it, to allow the Ukrainians to breed further. Hitler agreed. Only a few months before, in February 1942, Hitler had fumed about the mistakes that previous German colonizers had made: 'No sooner do we land in a colony than we install children's crèches, hospitals for the natives. All this fills me with rage.... The Russians don't grow old. They scarcely get beyond 50 or 60. What a ridiculous idea to vaccinate them! ...No vaccination for the Russians and no soap to get the dirt off them. But let them have all the vodka and tobacco they want.'

Now, after discussions with Bormann, and notwithstanding his desire to deny the Ukrainians other modern medical care, Hitler accepted that the local population should be encouraged to use contraceptives provided for them by the Nazis. But only weeks

before Bormann's eye-opening trip around the Ukrainian countryside a zealous Nazi official, acting no doubt on what he believed would be Hitler's wishes, had decided to ban contraceptives in the occupied territories, arguing that since they were evidence of sophisticated medical knowledge, the Führer would wish them to be denied to these 'natives'. Hitler fumed: 'If some idiot should actually try and carry out such a prohibition in the occupied East, he [Hitler] would personally shoot him to pieces. In the occupied Eastern territories a brisk trade in contraceptives shall not only be permitted but even encouraged, for one could have no interest in the excessive multiplication of the non-German population.'

The day after Hitler had uttered these words Bormann relayed the Führer's wish that there be a 'brisk trade in contraceptives' in the East to Rosenberg. (Bormann's memorandum also emphasized that 'German public health services shall under no circumstances be established in the occupied Eastern territories.') The administrators in Rosenberg's ministry were outraged, some complaining that the phrase 'brisk trade in contraceptives' should not be associated with the Führer. But at least Rosenberg's ministry was not ordered to

carry out these instructions. That fell to Koch, who was only too eager to add these racially inspired measures to his long and vindictive action plan against the Ukrainians.

The story of the contraceptives is instructive not just because it shows how obsessive Hitler and Bormann could be about such a matter of detail, but also because it demonstrates the power of Hitler's underlying racist belief. From his perspective, part of the reason for Operation Barbarossa was, indeed, to stop the Slavs 'breeding like vermin'.

For Aleksey Bris the tension inside him caused by the way the Germans were treating the Ukrainians – beatings and hangings in his local town were commonplace – finally burst out in dramatic fashion on 12 September 1942. It was a bright autumn day, and Bris was standing idly in a street near the centre of Horokhiv, watching as townspeople queued to buy the belongings of Jews whom the Germans had killed – pots and

ABOVE (left to right) Martin Bormann, Adolf Hitler, Erich Koch and Hitler's adjutant Schaub at Vinnitsa in late summer 1942. Koch's closeness to Bormann, together with his direct access to Hitler via his role as a Gauleiter, were to be of great assistance in his battle with Rosenberg.

OPPOSITE Adolf Hitler and Hermann Göring take a walk at Werewolf, Hitler's headquarters at Vinnitsa in the Ukraine, during the summer of 1942.

Aleksey Bris, the young Ukrainian who dared to stand up to the Germans.

pans and other kitchenware. But it wasn't this fact that prompted Bris to action. (When pressed on why he seemed so relaxed about both the Germans and the Ukrainian townspeople profiting from the murder of the local Jews, he replied: 'I don't think they thought much about *what* they were buying – they just thought about the chance of buying *anything*.') One of the locals tried to jump the queue and was beaten with a cane by one of the German soldiers supervising the sale. Something snapped inside Bris as he saw this fellow Ukrainian being whipped, and he grabbed the German policeman by the collar. 'How could you allow him to hit this person?' Bris shouted to members of the German administration who stood nearby.

The Germans stared in shock. Who was this 'inferior' who had dared lay his hand upon a member of the master race? Then a member of the German administration recovered himself and screamed '*Raus!*' ('Get out!') at Bris, who stayed still – he didn't know what to do. The German shouted again and then hit Bris with his own cane. And that was the moment Bris's life changed. He fought back. 'I had this kind of chivalrous knight idea...I felt on the edge of mental collapse...at that moment I wasn't afraid of the Germans. When you are hit like that, the emotions come first and you don't think about the consequences.' Bris darted forward, grabbed the cane from the German and pushed him over. Then he kicked him on the head. Another member of the German administration standing nearby made a grab for his pistol. As he fumbled to undo the straps on his holster, Bris started to run.

Meleti Semenyuk was among the townspeople who witnessed Bris's actions that day: 'I felt that he was a hero, especially because I knew that he used to work for the Germans.' As he watched the German policeman beat the queue-jumper, Semenyuk too was ready to react against them. 'I hated all of them. But Bris was the first man to act.'

The Germans mounted a massive search for Bris. They went straight to the house where he lived with his relatives and beat them severely before taking them to a concentration camp. They posted leaflets around the town offering a reward of 10,000 Reichsmarks for his capture. But Bris had escaped to the forest. Having once worked for the Germans, he was now determined to fight against them.

Bris's own personal history mirrors the experience of thousands of other disillusioned Ukrainians, though few began their resistance to the Germans in such a dramatic way. And since this link between the cruelty of the German civilian administration and the creation of a resistance movement seems clear, the result has been that men like Koch – as the physical embodiment of Hitler's sentiments – have become convenient scapegoats. Artillery officer Rüdiger von Reichert noticed that the 'friendly attitude' of the local population changed only 'when the effects of the civilian administration, which followed after the military administration, were felt. Naturally word got round very rapidly that in general they would behave as members of a master race and treat everyone like slaves and exploit them.' Former Panzer officer Walter Schaefer-Kehnert agrees: 'We came for them as a kind of liberator,' he says, 'liberating them from the Bolshevistic community system. My personal opinion is that the Nazis were too stupid to exploit that. You see, we could really have come as liberators but their [the Nazis'] idea that they were second-class human beings was ridiculous.... The Russians and the Ukrainians, they were

ABOVE A typical scene during the German occupation of Kharkov – women pull a cart containing all they possess.

OPPOSITE A young boy begs in the street in Kharkov. The German policy of feeding properly only those capable of productive work meant that this boy probably died of starvation.

people like we were ourselves, with a great feeling for human dignity.'

Many other German soldiers expressed a similar view, claiming that the maltreatment of the civilian population in the occupied territories was the responsibility of Nazi administrators such as Koch. As a result, they exonerated the German Army from blame. But that's not what actually happened – for not all of the Ukraine was in the hands of Koch. Whilst the majority of it was in his Reichskommissariat, Galicia and Volhynia in the west were incorporated into the General Government under his fellow Nazi administrator Hans Frank, and the territory nearest the front line, including the eastern Ukrainian city of Kharkov, came under the jurisdiction of the German military authorities. And that city's population suffered more under the German military administration than Bris's home town of Horokhiv did under Koch's rule.

The military rulers of Kharkov were responsible, in the winter of 1942–3, for a famine in which thousands died (the precise number who died in the German occupation of Kharkov will probably never be known – one estimate is about 100,000). Whilst the Army requisitioned huge quantities of food for themselves, the vast majority of the population received nothing to eat at all from the Germans. The soldiers watched as the weakest members of the population – most often women, children and the elderly – simply starved to death.

'They didn't pay much attention to people dying,' says Inna Gavrilchenko, talking of the attitude of the German military administrators. 'They took it easy. I don't think they were shocked.' Inna, a teenaged girl during the occupation, witnessed how the townspeople tried to survive: 'First they killed dogs and ate them. But the dogs didn't last long. So they ate rats, pigeons, crows.' When the animals ran out, the most desperate started to eat human flesh. 'There were some people who excavated fresh graves to get the bodies. And they boiled them and cooked them in all possible ways. They made meat jelly out of bones and ate some cakes with human flesh.'

The German military administration didn't just give the non-working inhabitants nothing to eat, they also sealed Kharkov as a security measure, preventing the townspeople from being able to

barter for food with the local farmers. As a result, Inna's beloved father died of starvation in front of her. Almost delirious with hunger herself, she sat talking to his body for eight days in their flat before a neighbour came and helped prepare the body for burial: 'For a very long time I had a fear that they buried him alive. Sometimes [sitting with her father when he was dead] I heard sighs. Maybe it was just gases in his body as a result of decay...I don't know.'

Inna believed she too was going to die of starvation. But she was lucky. A neighbour who worked in a German canteen used to take the water in which she had washed the Germans' dirty dishes, boil it up and make her drink it – there were occasional remnants of food floating in it. Inna also worked for a short time as an errand-girl in a German meat factory in the town. Sometimes the Germans who worked there would give her a scrap of bone or a bottle of blood: 'With blood,' she says, 'you can make an omelette...just like you make scrambled eggs, but without the eggs.'

When a blood omelette wasn't possible, she ate what she could find in the nearby woods within the city limits: 'Have you ever tried the bark of a birch tree?... It is sweetish. And you can try the leaves and young twigs of jasmine. There are a lot of edible things that you hate to think of today.'

Heartbreaking as Inna Gavrilchenko's story is, there are even worse examples of the suffering the German Army brought to Kharkov – and many of them relate to the maltreatment of children. Anatoly Reva was only six years old when the Germans arrived. His torment began when some prisoners of war were temporarily held behind his family house. Anatoly's father, seeing their suffering, threw food over the fence to them. The Germans shouted at him to stop, but he didn't hear, so they shot him dead. As a result of the shock, the little boy's mother lost her sight and was taken for treatment to a hospital that Anatoly could not find. So in March 1942, without any relations to care for him, he found himself alone.

He began to beg in the streets. But since as a child he was what the Germans called an *unnützer Esser* (useless eater), his prospects were bleak. Then his fortune seemed to change. One day he was befriended by a woman who took him to an orphanage in Kharkov. He slept that night on a bed of hay and the next morning awoke and waited for some breakfast – but the orphanage had no food that day or the next. The children were fed on scraps just twice a week. So, to survive, they had to run into the forest and scavenge. 'I was so hungry that I was eating nuts,' says Reva, 'and these nuts were poisonous, but I had to eat them because my stomach required some kind of food. Other children ate grass or leaves.'

Children in the orphanage regularly died of hunger, most often at night. But starvation was not the only cause of death in that institution. From time to time German soldiers came, looking for anyone who was circumcised, anyone who was Jewish. Once, Anatoly watched as a Jewish boy was discovered and taken away to be shot.

The selection of these Jewish children would almost certainly have been done by the SS or other security forces. But for the most part the town was home to 'ordinary' soldiers of the German Army. Once, Anatoly approached a group of these men and, his desperation overcoming his fear, begged for some food. One of them said, 'Hold on a minute' and reappeared moments later with a 'bag full of excrement'. 'They didn't have any kind of human feelings,' says Anatoly. 'They didn't feel sorry for children.'

It was administrators from the German Army, not Nazis like Koch, who presided over this nightmare world and orchestrated the famine. But the guilt and responsibility of the German Army for the savage way in which civilians were treated during the war in the East does not stop there. Hitler had ordered that during any retreat 'every place of inhabitation must be burnt down and destroyed without consideration for the population'. And that is just what the German Army did. After the war many former Wehrmacht soldiers tried to pretend that it was only the SS and the killing squads of the Einsatzgruppen who had carried out barbarous actions in the East. Today, we know that to be a lie. Academic researchers, studying the detailed records of individual Wehrmacht units in the East, have shown in recent years that, especially in the rear areas, the committing of atrocities against the civilian population

OPPOSITE Inna Gavrilchenko, who survived the occupation of Kharkov by eating blood omelettes and birch tree bark.

OVERLEAF Hitler photographed in 1942 with his generals and, in the black hat, Ferdinand Porsche, the car designer. By now the Holocaust was in full swing, and even the non-Jewish population of the German-occupied territories had been reduced to the status of slaves.

was widespread. And the evidence against the Wehrmacht is not contained just in documents – it comes from the testimony of surviving German soldiers themselves.

Walter Schaefer-Kehnert's Panzer group participated in the burning down of Soviet villages as part of the German scorched earth policy in the wake of their repositioning after the Battle of Moscow: 'You see, the soldiers disliked it utterly. They said better to have a real battle than to burn the houses of the civilian population, so we were very reluctant to do so.' When asked what happened to the people whose houses he burnt, he said: 'Well, they had to look somewhere else, going to the next village or wherever they could.' But surely the next village might have been burnt as well? 'Sure,' he replied, 'but you were busy enough looking after yourself....'

Walter Mauth, a German infantryman with the 30th Division, also took part in this scorched earth policy later in the war: 'I never noticed anybody bothering to have a look inside the house to see whether there was a sick woman or anybody else in there. The houses were simply brutally shot at and burnt down. That's just the way it was. Nobody cared. There was no consideration – they were "sub-human creatures" after all, weren't they?' As part of the rearguard of his unit, Mauth watched as his comrades committed murder. 'I witnessed how they shot into the houses.... But since they were Russian, it did not matter. On the contrary, you were even decorated – the more people you shot, the higher was the decoration you received. That's the truth.'

As he reflects today on how the German Army behaved in the East, he confesses that 'personally, I consider the acts that have been committed a crime, then and now – in retrospect I consider it a damn scandal! I would like to pass on my experience, as far as I am able, to ensure that everybody knows what they will let themselves in for [in war]. They will become a criminal.'

Wolfgang Horn of the 10th Panzer Division personally ordered the burning down of a Russian village in a reprisal action. Crucial to his ability to deny women and children shelter was his overall belief about the sort of people he was fighting. 'One divided Europe into three areas,' he says, 'Europe A, B and C. So Russia was Europe C – the lowest standard of all. England or Germany or France were Europe A and Poland maybe Europe B.' He didn't think the Russians were 'as civilized as we are.... They were not accustomed to normal behaviour, like coming in on time and doing one's work efficiently, as we were in Germany.' All this meant that to burn down a Russian village was of no great consequence to him. 'Burning down a civilized house' would have been very different. As he saw it, a Russian house was primitive and not of much value.

The last of these four witnesses who bear testimony to atrocities committed by the German Army is Albert Schneider, who was a mechanic in the 201st Assault Gun Battalion. He told us how, as his unit passed through a Russian village, a comrade of his stole a pig from one of the peasants. The owner of the pig objected and started to wail in protest. So his comrade drew his pistol and shot him. 'I was unable to say anything about it,' says Schneider. 'Perhaps I was too much of a coward. I'm not all that brave.'

Not only did Schneider witness the aftermath of atrocities committed by individual Wehrmacht soldiers (on top of a heap of corpses in one village he saw the body of a woman with a German bayonet thrust into her vagina), but his unit, under instructions from its commander, systematically perpetrated a war crime. Staying overnight in a remote Russian village, his unit garaged some of their vehicles in a barn. During the night one of the engines blew up. Next morning, the officer commanding his unit ordered all the men from the village – some as young as 12 – to be gathered together. Then they were told to run away from the German soldiers, and as they scattered they were shot in the back. This all took place 'without any investigation at all as to what had actually happened', says Schneider. 'Why, it might have been that the engines overheated because they were Maybach engines which tend to overheat very quickly.' The officer who ordered this terrible reprisal should not be thought of today as unique. At the time he would have felt his actions were justified by the special powers, for use only in the East, given to him by the German Army (see page 30). (General Halder had asked for a provision to be inserted in the infamous Barbarossa Directive of May 1941 which allowed a commanding officer to order the burning of villages and the killing of some of the inhabitants if he believed they were supporting Soviet partisans.)

Having witnessed theft and mass murder, Albert Schneider also admits that rape was commonplace. Many Wehrmacht soldiers still say today that sexual molestation of the local women was out of the question – not least because these women were, the German soldiers were repeatedly told, members of an 'inferior' race and such an action would have been judged a 'race crime' and severely punished. But that was not Schneider's experience. He saw one of his comrades take a Russian woman into a barn and heard the woman scream as she was raped. After it was over his comrade boasted, 'Well, I showed that one!'

'But that was not an isolated incident,' says Schneider. 'There were several cases in this village in particular when women were actually raped...it was well known throughout the ranks that things like this were going on. And nobody said a word about it.... I once

A series of photographs taken during a German raid on a village in the occupied territories. ABOVE A Soviet family submit to having their picture taken by the German photographer.

BELOW The displaced villagers cower as their homes burn. Notice how few men there are in the crowd: any man of military age was regarded by the Germans as a possible partisan.

ABOVE The Germans use a flame-thrower to raze houses to the ground. Villages were destroyed either in a reprisal action against partisans or to deny enemy troops shelter.

BELOW The Germans lead away their booty. The planning stages of Operation Barbarossa had envisaged the German soldiers 'living off the land' – a euphemism for simple theft.

asked a sergeant why nothing was being done about it. And he said: "Because half the army would have to face trial!" In my opinion that says it all.'

The mass of the civilian population of the occupied areas could therefore be violated and oppressed by any combination of German agencies – the Army, the SS, the Einsatzgruppen (who, by the autumn of 1941, were shooting every Jew in the occupied Eastern territories, including women and children) and the civilian administration under fanatical racists like Koch. All of them are responsible both for the escalation of the suffering of the civilian population and for helping to create greater resistance to the German occupation.

On the Soviet side, Stalin had called for a partisan movement to rise and fight against the Germans as early in the war as 3 July 1941. In a speech made that day he announced: 'Conditions must be made unbearable for the enemy and his collaborators – they must be pursued and annihilated wherever they are.'

Hitler's response to Stalin's call is instructive. 'This partisan war in turn has its advantages,' Hitler said. 'It gives us a chance to eliminate anyone who turns against us.' This meant, of course, that the suffering of the occupied population could only increase. Since neither Hitler nor Stalin was held in check by moral considerations, neither were the forces they controlled – such as the Soviet partisans or the German forces who tried to track them down. In most guerrilla wars, such as that in Vietnam, one side (in that case the Americans) is trying to preserve the status quo. In this partisan war neither side wanted to keep the status quo – the Germans wanted to reorder the occupied areas to create their new, racially inspired empire, and the Soviet partisans wanted not just to disrupt the Germans but to impose their will on the local population as well. Part of the role of these partisans was to root out 'collaborators' and remind the indigenous population that Stalinist terror could still operate even in German-occupied territory.

The partisan movement didn't develop systematically. The first phase, from the outbreak of the war until the spring of 1942, was characterized by failure. Despite Stalin's rhetoric, the Soviet Union was not prepared to fight a guerrilla war. The concept of 'defence through attack' – the idea that any future war should be carried out on the enemy's soil – had, in theory, rendered partisan warfare unnecessary. And Stalin's natural suspiciousness meant that he was innately ill-disposed to the idea of armed bands operating behind enemy lines far from the control of Moscow. That, plus the belief in many quarters in the early

OPPOSITE Both Germans and Soviets followed a policy of 'scorched earth', and neither practised any restraint in the bombardment of towns choked with civilians. This landscape was the result of such actions.

BELOW A mother and her children watch as their village burns. A German attitude that these homes were 'not civilized' contributed to the ease with which villages could be destroyed.

months of the war that the Germans would win, combined with the hopes of those, like Aleksey Bris, that the Germans would prove sympathetic conquerors, meant initially that Soviet partisans were isolated. The massive German anti-partisan actions of early 1942, such as Operation Hanover, marked the partisans' lowest ebb. But with Stalin's growing support, and motivated by the belief that Germany might conceivably be defeated, the

A woman pleads with the photographer as her home is burnt to the ground.

movement began to grow in effectiveness. The actual number of Soviet partisans engaged in the fight against the Germans is notoriously difficult to estimate. One of the latest calculations is that at the end of 1941 there were 2000 partisan detachments giving a total of 72,000 partisans, and that by the summer of 1944 around 500,000 partisans were fighting the Germans. (Communication with Moscow was spasmodic – for much of the war 90 per cent of the partisans had no radio contact with their own side.)

Mikhail Timoshenko was one of Stalin's Soviet partisans – a member of an NKVD special unit. He conducted the fight against the Germans and the 'traitors' in the occupied civilian population with a ruthlessness that the Soviet leader would have approved of. As a general rule he ordered any German prisoners whom his unit captured to be shot. 'What could we do with them?' says Timoshenko. 'Release them so they could kill us again?' He would ask for volunteers from amongst his men to do the actual shooting, and there was never a shortage of willing killers. 'You know they considered them as enemies they had to destroy,' says Timoshenko. 'Understand that these people had had their houses burnt down – with their parents still inside them. These men were vengeful.'

Living behind the lines, mundane considerations, such as where to get enough food, became a major problem. The partisans occasionally had parachute drops of supplies, but for the most part they lived off the land – or off the Germans. Timoshenko always snatched the packs of the Germans he had shot 'because in them, especially those belonging to the divisions that had come from Europe, there was rum and chocolate. There were salami tins! They were stuffed with food and we needed to be fed.'

When there were no Germans to ambush, the partisans took food from the local villagers. And that could be a major cause of conflict. Ivan Treskovski was a teenager living with his family in a ramshackle farmhouse on the edge of the village of Usyazha deep in the Belorussian countryside. He remembers how he cowered upstairs and listened when the Soviet partisans came to pay a call on his father: 'They'd be drunk, drunk!' he says. 'They'd take our fat, our chickens and our clothing. They'd take it to another village and sell it or change it for vodka – that's what they did.' On one occasion in the winter of 1942 he heard the partisans shout at his father, 'Give us some bacon fat or we'll kill you!' For the locals in this region life became a daily round of terror. In the daytime there was always the fear that the Germans would come, and during the night they were at risk from the partisans.

Whilst German lines of communication did risk disruption at their hands, the greatest impact the partisans had was on the lives of the occupied population. Stalin himself authorized his partisans to kill any locals who were helping the Germans. Mikhail Timoshenko admits that he and his band of partisans killed those who they thought had collaborated. Indeed, so strong was his reputation for shooting 'traitors' that one of the German propaganda newspapers printed a caricature of him. Underneath there was the caption: 'This is the leader of the partisan movement who destroys everything he gets his hands on: he steals cows and robs collective farms.' Timoshenko remembers that his hands were shown 'covered in blood'. He felt this attack was 'unfair': 'They'd written that I killed local traitors. Well, there were instances when we did kill traitors. We killed any of the population who helped the Germans. But they said that I shot people who wouldn't give me their cattle. That's nonsense, of course.'

These partisan groups made their own laws, and Timoshenko admits that part of his job was, as Stalin would have wished, to deal with those 'who had lost the conviction that Soviet power would be victorious'. If he suspected a particular villager was a 'traitor', he would send two men to his house at night to snatch him. They would interrogate him and then, as was most likely, believing him to be an informer, they would shoot him. 'There were no courts,' says Timoshenko. 'There was no power other than my own.... It was essentially a terror, but a terror against dishonourable people.'

The potential for abuse in such a system is, of course, enormous. Ivan Treskovski recalls that there were villagers who might, out of spite, tell the partisans that someone had links with the Germans – and then the one who was denounced was murdered. As he puts it: 'Whoever had the gun was the master and did whatever he wanted.'

Eastern Belorussia, with its thick forest close to isolated villages, was ideal country for partisan activities, and teenaged Nadezhda Nefyodova and her family discovered personally how they could bring their murderous vengeance down on anyone they chose. One night in November 1942 the local partisans came to the tiny village of Prilepy, just outside Minsk, and murdered her sister and her husband. There was no explanation – the partisans didn't need to justify their murder. The deaths led to speculation that perhaps one of them had been seen talking to the Germans. Then, since other people were also killed that night, a theory grew that the whole village had in some way offended the partisan leader. In a civilized society someone is accused, convicted and punished. In this shadowy world of suspicion and revenge villagers were first murdered and then speculation grew about what crime they might conceivably have committed.

Nadezhda Nefyodova's family took in and hid the murdered couple's two small children, who were little more than babies and had been cowering underneath the bed while their parents were murdered. But the local partisans seemed to want to kill the children as well, because now they pursued the whole of Nadezhda's family. During the day it was safe for them to stay at their house, but at night, when the partisans might come, the family scattered. Her father slept concealed in hay at the other side of the village, whilst Nadezhda, her mother and the two little children all went to other relatives in nearby villages. The next day they would reassemble and begin work in the fields

around their home, trying to grow enough food to survive.

The local partisans were led by Petr Sankovich, a committed Communist who had been the chief vet for the area before the war. His most faithful lieutenant was Efim Goncharov, the local headmaster and a member of the district party committee. The lawless atmosphere of the time is captured in this official report from another Belorussian partisan, Vladimir Lashuk, dated May 1942: 'I served with Goncharov, and we completed a whole series of attacks on the Fascist occupiers, turncoats, traitors and other German supporters.' And, of course, they themselves decided who was a 'turncoat' or a 'traitor'.

But Nadezhda Nefyodova and her family didn't suffer only at the hands of the Soviet partisans. In March 1943, a drunken Soviet partisan shot at a German plane from just outside Usyazha, Nadezhda's village. Reprisals followed. The next day Stukhas dive-bombed the village, and then the German-controlled police arrived. Most of the villagers hid in the nearby woods as soon as the bombing started, but Nadezhda's brother Siyonas stayed behind. Bravely, he climbed on to the wooden roof of their house and tried to put out the fire caused by the incendiaries. He managed to save the house but it cost him his life because he was still in the village when the German police arrived. They set fire to the barn in which he took refuge and then, as he emerged, shot him. Twenty-seven out of 28 houses in the village were destroyed in the German reprisal attack and 29 villagers died.

'Do you know how hard it was to live in the middle of all those garrisons?' Nadezhda asks. 'Germans during the day, and at night those bandits would arrive. You had to be afraid of all of them because none of them came with good intentions. And if you protested, what did it mean to them to kill you? You were a mere fly! You were living all the time – from morning till evening and evening till morning – in such tension.... You didn't know what tomorrow would bring, so you just lived for that day...just for that

hour.' Surprisingly, given the Western perception of Hitler's war in the East, she concluded by voicing her view that as far as she was concerned it had been the Soviet partisans – not the Germans – who had been the more 'terrifying' enemy: 'Of course the partisans were crueller – they came at night and to their own kind.'

Petr Sankovich, the local partisan leader, was killed in an ambush with German forces in February 1944, but Efim Goncharov survived the war, was awarded a medal and became chairman of the district committee. Whilst there are still calls for the prosecution of remaining German war criminals, it is worth remembering the criminals on the Soviet side who prospered long after the war and were never punished. 'If my sister and her husband had lived, then all our lives would have been different,' says Nadezhda today. 'There remains an after-taste of spite in my heart.'

ABOVE Efim Goncharov was a teacher before the war, but during the conflict became a notorious partisan suspected of the murder of Nadezhda Nefyodova's sister and her husband. After the war he received a medal.
OPPOSITE Nadezhda Nefyodova: her sister was killed by the partisans, her brother by the Germans.

Nadezhda Nefyodova and her family in Belorussia lived between the Germans and the partisans and suffered cruelty at the hands of each. But in nearby German-occupied Ukraine there were those who were caught in an even tighter trap. For here there was a third force, the Ukrainian Nationalist partisans, committed to fighting both the Germans *and* the Soviet partisans.

Meleti Semenyuk fought with the Ukrainian Nationalists (the Ukrainska Povstanska Armiia or UPA). The disillusionment caused by the harsh German rule offered an opportunity to fight for an independent Ukraine. To the Soviet partisans, and to Stalin, they were as much an enemy as the Germans. 'The aim of the Red partisans was to eliminate our movement so that they could come back to a clean area,' says Semenyuk. 'And those partisans – like animals – I cannot describe them.' Stories of atrocities committed by the Soviet partisans (often long after the war with the Germans was over, as Stalin ordered the Ukraine to be 'cleansed') are commonplace in the Ukraine. A secret Soviet Interior Ministry report acknowledges that the Soviet forces committed 'anarchic and oppressive actions against local citizens'. In one example of such an action, the report describes how an undercover Soviet group which had infiltrated the UPA 'brutally tortured a 62-year-old man and his two daughters'.

After escaping from his village, Aleksey Bris joined the UPA. He remembers the cruelty of the conflict with the Soviet partisans: 'The Germans just killed us, but with the Red partisans the bestialities were different. Some of them were cutting the ears off our members. In rare cases they have this Asian way of torturing people – cutting your ears and tongue off. I don't know if they did this to people who were still alive, but these events happened quite often. It's sadism which exists in every system. The Germans just hanged people, but I never saw anything like tortured bodies. But, of course, we were quite cruel...we didn't take any prisoners of war and they didn't take any prisoners either, so we killed each other. That was natural.'

The secretive and arbitrary way in which the partisans most often conducted their fight, together with the fact that the majority of atrocities against the local population were never reported for fear of further reprisal, means that it will never be possible to

Villagers seek refuge in a forest. Their white flag afforded little protection as neither side in this war regarded civilians as 'innocent'.

quantify accurately the precise numbers of crimes the partisans committed. Nor is it easy to assess the damage these partisan movements actually inflicted on their German occupiers, for their impact was as much psychological as physical. Mere figures for the number of Germans killed by partisans during the war (one estimate is about 50,000) underestimate the effect of their presence on the German infrastructure. This plaintive letter from a Herr Schenk, who ran a mining and steel company in eastern Ukraine, gives some sense of how the Germans could be affected in practical terms by the virtual civil war that erupted during their occupation. He writes, in April 1943, that around him are '1. Partisans, who are nothing but Bolsheviks...' and '2. There is a large number of national Ukrainian partisans who are also located in these forests...'. He sums up the situation between these two groups succinctly, for as well as attacking him, 'Groups 1 and 2 are also fighting against each other.' In addition, 'There are so-called bandits...who are disrupting the main-line traffic.' In this morass 'travelling by car is today extremely dangerous'. One local police officer remarked to Schenk as he began a journey, 'f you're lucky, you'll make it through.' Schenk concludes his letter by writing: 'The economic situation is suffering greatly under these conditions to the point that there is no German administration left at all in many regions.'

Hitler's solution to these problems was simple: more brutality, more killings, more oppression. This view was shared by the Wehrmacht Commander-in-Chief in the Ukraine, who reported as early as December 1941 that 'The fight against the partisans succeeds only if the population realizes that the partisans and their sympathizers sooner or later are killed.... Death by strangulation inspires fear more particularly...only measures that can frighten the population more than the terror of partisans can lead to success. The Army Group recommends resort to such measures as needed.'

But, as with most Nazi policies that involved individual discretion, the anti-partisan policy was anything but consistent. Local commanders were free to a large extent to determine their own actions – some even did deals with the partisans in their area. Führer Directive No. 46 of August 1942 attempted to clarify the way the German forces should deal with the partisan problem. But it served only to muddy the waters still further. On the one hand it recognized that the cooperation of the local population was important in the fight against the partisans, but it also warned against confidence in the local population being 'misplaced'. This one directive shows in microcosm the inability of Hitler and the Nazi hard-liners to accept the idea that the population they were dealing with were proper human beings. They knew they needed the locals to help against the partisans, but they also knew that a necessary precondition of gaining their help was to treat them decently – something that went against their basic ideological beliefs.

Yet it was clear by the end of the summer of 1942 that this policy of harsh repression was not getting the desired results. An alternative was suggested by Colonel Reinhard

Gehlen, head of the German Army's Intelligence Agency for the East, who concluded in a report in November 1942: 'If the population rejects the partisans and lends its full support to the struggle against them, no partisan problem will exist.' The resulting debate mirrored that between Koch and Rosenberg on the Ukrainian political question. This time it was a few army commanders, such as Gehlen, who argued for partnership with the local population against the partisans. Gehlen called for captured Soviet partisans to be treated as 'normal' prisoners of war – and in some cases this was done in Army Group Centre (who faced the Red Army east of Smolensk) in 1943. He also mounted propaganda leaflet campaigns against some partisan groups with varying results.

Unsurprisingly, Hitler did not share Gehlen's views. The Führer had concluded that 'only where the struggle against the partisan nuisance was begun and carried out with ruthless brutality have successes been achieved'. Just like the whole war on the Eastern Front, the struggle against the partisans was viewed by Hitler as 'a struggle of total annihilation of one side or the other'. The natural consequence of this attitude was that, despite the best efforts of a few soldiers like Gehlen, the brutality escalated. If each side believes that the only way to fight fear is 'with more fear', as Vladimir Ogryzko put it in the context of the battle for Moscow, then the only limit on cruelty is the human imagination.

Some of the harshest German anti-partisan actions of all were launched in eastern Belorussia in the summer of 1943 – a few months after the 'invincible' German Sixth Army had been destroyed at Stalingrad and whilst the Red Army fought back the German summer advance at the Battle of Kursk. During this 'cleansing' in the countryside around Minsk, on 22 July, German units came to the tiny village of Maksimoky. They burst into the house of teenager Aleksandr Mikhailovski and awoke both him and his deaf and dumb brother. On the dusty road outside, as dawn broke, the Germans assembled eight villagers, including Aleksandr and his brother. They tied their hands behind their backs and ordered them to walk down the road, with the Germans following about 50 metres behind.

OPPOSITE Rare photographs of a German execution in the occupied territories. The prisoners are marched to a secluded place, lined up before a pit, and shot. Who the victims are is unknown. The Germans may well have described them simply as 'partisans' – a catch-all term which allowed them to kill anyone they did not like the look of.

Aleksandr knew what this meant, for the Germans had used this same technique in nearby villages. Partisans had planted mines on many of the roads in the area, and the Germans used the locals as human mine detectors. (This kind of sadism was not

uncommon. Curt von Gottberg, the SS-Obergruppenführer who, during 1943, conducted another huge anti-partisan action called Operation Kottbus on the eastern border of Belorussia, reported that 'approximately two to three thousand local people were blown up in the clearing of the minefields'.)

'Your heart turned to stone and you went to a living death,' says Mikhailovski of his treatment at German hands. 'The people went along just like they were already dead. They knew that only despair and tears awaited us.' Their dilemma as they walked along the road was a stark one. 'Whenever we felt there was something suspicious, we'd try to avoid it. But we knew that if we avoided a mine and it blew up a German behind us, then we'd die all the same because they'd shoot you.'

The Germans forced them along the dusty road for eight hours as they walked nearly 30 kilometres to the next village. The terror was constant: 'Our mouths were dry and because of our tears we couldn't see the road.' But they were lucky. On this stretch of road there were no mines. At the end of this ordeal they owed their lives to another piece of good fortune. The Germans were about to kill them, but the locals protested vehemently to the army commander that these were not 'bandits' but innocent villagers and their lives were spared.

An insight into the mentality of those German soldiers who had to grapple with the partisan problem is given by Peter von der Groeben, the Operations Officer of Army Group Centre and its most senior staff officer after the Commander-in-Chief. He acknowledges that the partisans 'were conducting a highly successful war against our reinforcement troops. On the railways, the roads, everywhere, blowing up the railway lines, destroying roads, attacking columns.' In addition he 'assumes' that, since his soldiers were angry when they saw German columns attacked and mutilated, then 'if they captured a partisan village, I am quite convinced that their behaviour wasn't very gentle. I assume they more or less killed everybody they came across there.'

Confirmation of this behaviour comes from Carlheinz Behnke, a soldier now with the 4th SS-Police Panzergrenadier Division. His section came upon some 20 or so German soldiers from his own unit who had been left behind wounded, and who now had been murdered and mutilated by Soviet forces 'in the most bestial manner – their ears had been cut off, their eyes had been gouged out and their genitals had been cut off'. The commander of his detachment gave the order that any civilians still present in the area were to be shot as a reprisal, 'without any consideration being given to the women or even the children'. Behnke thought this order 'logical and correct', and he himself participated in the consequent killing of civilians. A sleigh was crossing the ice about 400 metres away from him and he, along with his fellow soldiers, fired at it and saw the three occupants topple over. 'I don't know whether they were children, women...obviously you look at these things differently nowadays...but it was a moment which is impossible to describe and nobody who didn't witness it can understand it, I think.'

Behnke admits that his unit became incensed and vented their anger in indiscriminate murder. Only after 24 hours, their blood lust sated, did they regain some control. Their wild emotional state, which Behnke, in common with Peter von der Groeben, sees as some kind of justification for the subsequent committing of atrocities, is in fact the reverse – an example of how units of the German Army lost their discipline and permitted themselves to behave like crazed bandits.

We traced a revealing report read and initialled by Peter von der Groeben in his capacity as Operations Officer (Ia) of Army Group Centre about the German anti-partisan Operation Otto. It lists around 2000 'partisans' and their 'helpers' killed, but it details only 30 rifles and a handful of other weapons recovered from them. This extraordinary disparity, even today, does not surprise him. 'Look, the partisans must have had the necessary weapons – otherwise they could not have done anything to us,' he argues. And in response to the argument that this might be evidence that German troops were killing indiscriminately, he replies: 'I can't

Carlheinz Behnke in SS uniform – a representative of one of the most feared Nazi organizations of all.

remember. As I said, the troops' fury was immense. Well, I would imagine that they also killed some innocent people. But who could tell who was innocent?' When pressed, he would only accept: 'Well, if the counter-actions themselves did go over the top, I think they were regarded as unpleasant but necessary counter-measures which were, of course, also meant to be a deterrent.'

Similar discrepancies between the number of 'partisans' killed and the number of weapons recovered occurred in the SS statistics for their own anti-partisan operations. When Himmler was asked why this was happening he replied: 'You appear not to know that these bandits destroy their weapons to play the innocent and so avoid death.' Not surprisingly, these harsh measures did not eradicate the partisan problem. The German Army High Command conceded in 1943 that they had not been able to rid the occupied territories of these 'bandits'.

A Soviet family flees across the snow. It was villagers like these whom Carlheinz Behnke's unit turned upon.

It is simplistic to state that the Nazis' racism was the only cause of the cruelty of the partisan war. Other factors clearly contributed to the escalation of the brutality, not least the vast area that the Germans had to control, the despair felt by many German soldiers that the war as a whole was not going in a way that favoured them, and the ruthless way in which Stalin's partisans could terrorize the locals and murder and mutilate captured German soldiers. But it is true to say that to stand a chance of eliminating the partisan threat, the Germans needed the cooperation of the indigenous population, and it was Nazi racist beliefs that made such assistance impossible.

It's easy to argue that this failure was simply another of Hitler's tactical mistakes. 'If only he had been more flexible,' the argument goes, 'and treated the inhabitants of the occupied territories with the basic respect due to all human beings, then the partisan war would not have escalated as it did.' But even to suggest this possibility is to misunderstand the nature of the whole war in the East. Hitler could never have moderated his policy towards the occupied territories. These racist beliefs were at the core of his being. They were almost how he defined himself. There were no circumstances in which Hitler would give up his vision of the new German Empire. Indeed, as the war progressed, far from doubting these central convictions, he became reconfirmed in his view that he was right. If the policy of treating the people of the East as 'sub-humans' was failing, then it was always the fault of other people around him – these 'vain, cowardly wretches' – who were not pursuing the policy of persecution with sufficient zeal.

Against the background of the growing partisan threat, Hitler set about trying, once more, to win the war on the battlefield. Now the Germans would advance south-east in a campaign that would be decided at a place then little known outside the Soviet Union – a city called Stalingrad.

CHAPTER

3

LEARNING HOW
TO WIN

T he year 1942 was one of transformation on the Eastern Front. At the start of it the Red Army was grappling with the Germans at the gates of Moscow. By the end of it the mighty German 6th Army was on its knees at Stalingrad.

It is easy, then, to characterize this as the year when the Soviets made the Germans pay for the arrogance of the original Barbarossa plan; to see this 12-month period as the time when a combination of the vast reserves of population from which the Red Army could draw, military aid from Britain and the USA, and the tanks and artillery from Soviet factories which had been dismantled in the face of the German advance and reconstructed far behind the front line, resulted in an inevitable change of fortune for Stalin and the Soviet Union. In short, it is easy to regard 1942 as the year when, day by inexorable day, the inevitability of a Soviet victory became obvious to the world.

But to judge that year in such a way would be a mistake. Instead, what the history of 1942 demonstrates is that, despite all the foreign help, all the manpower at their disposal, all the output of their factories, the Soviet Union could still have lost the war against the Germans. Both Stalin and the Red Army had to change the way they conducted the fight – and in the process, they had to learn from the enemy.

The Red Army performed badly in the first months of 1942 after the Battle of Moscow, and Stalin was the man most responsible. On 5 January he announced to the Stavka (the Soviet High Command) a plan almost as over-ambitious and contemptuous of the enemy as Hitler's original Barbarossa plan had been. Instead of concentrating the resources of the Red Army on one point of attack, Stalin proposed that they should advance on *all* fronts. In the north they would push to relieve

OPPOSITE Red Army soldiers in house-to-house fighting in Stalingrad in 1942. Their ability to wage this new kind of warfare – the antithesis of Blitzkrieg – on the Eastern Front was to prove crucial.

Leningrad, in front of Moscow they would attack Army Group Centre, and in the south they would confront the Germans in the Ukraine and the Crimea. In 1941 Stalin had demonstrated his military incompetence when it came to defence; now, at the start of 1942, he was showing his weakness as a commander in attack. Zhukov spotted the plan's flaws and said so. Nikolai Voznesensky, the economist, pointed out the grave logistical problems that would result from such an over-arching campaign, but was ridiculed as a man who 'only ever mentioned problems'. Against such protests the Soviet offensive began.

Not surprisingly, the Red Army made little progress as it attempted simultaneously to take on the Germans on all fronts, but at least there were no disastrous defeats. However, all that was to change when Stalin ordered a new offensive in the south, around the Ukrainian city of Kharkov, to begin in May 1942. The General Staff view was that the Red Army should be much less ambitious and consolidate its position around Moscow. But Stalin wanted action. 'Don't let us sit down in defence,' he stated baldly as he endorsed Marshal Timoshenko's plan for a major campaign. (Timoshenko, the offensive's main proponent and a comrade of Stalin's from the civil war, had previously seen his army encircled in 1941 by the Germans at Smolensk.)

Boris Vitman was an officer in the Soviet 6th Army and took part in the ill-fated Kharkov offensive of May 1942. At headquarters he saw that 'those who were planning the operation were certain that it would be completed successfully and the mood was very cheerful…the idea was that by 1943 the war would be finished.' Vitman noticed that the offensive was ambitiously called 'The campaign for the complete and final liberation of the Ukraine against the Nazi invaders'.

Stalin believed that the Germans' major campaign that year would be mounted in front of Moscow, and the Kharkov plan was based on that assumption. By attacking in the south, the Red Army hoped to disrupt the German preparations further north and strike the enemy at their weakest point. Unfortunately for the Soviets, their assessment of the German intention was wrong. The Germans were indeed planning a major offensive – but not on the Moscow axis. Instead they intended to attack through the Ukraine towards the south-east of the Soviet Union. Thus the Red Army unwittingly attacked the Germans

OPPOSITE Stalin ponders his next step. And in the spring of 1942 that was to be the ill-judged Kharkov offensive.

at the very place where they were preparing their own build-up. But even so, the Red Army still had superiority in numbers against the Germans for the forthcoming offensive – at least three Red Army soldiers to every two German ones, with the ratio even more favourable to the Soviets at the concentrated points of attack.

'On 12 May 1942, early in the morning, large numbers of artillery were lined up – so long that you couldn't see an end to them,' says Boris Vitman, who took part in the initial advance. 'The morning was misty, the sky was overcast, and this was good because it prevented German planes from seeing our divisions. All of a sudden you could hear a terrible noise. The earth was shaking. All the cannons opened fire simultaneously and this cannonade went on for more than an hour. Then when the cannonade stopped, the order came, "Go ahead!" and we advanced. Seeing such big power, such superiority, we were so inspired, we were going ahead thinking that victory was in our hands.'

Such optimism was misplaced. Anticipating an attack, the Germans had withdrawn and the mighty Soviet artillery barrage had been worthless. 'When we reached the German line, we saw that the defences were empty,' says Boris Vitman. 'There was not a single German dead body. There were only destroyed mock cannons. It was all a simulation of the German defence line, which in fact had been abandoned long ago. And we went on and on without meeting any resistance. We kept marching and marching. We did not give much thought to the fact that there were no Germans around. We thought we were marching towards Berlin.'

But, as Vitman and his men were about to discover, they had been lured into a German trap. 'On the outskirts of Kharkov all of a sudden our attack faced very strong resistance as the Germans had prepared a powerful defensive line. Our attack was choked.' And then their predicament grew worse. 'There was the rumour that, as we were advancing, the Germans struck on the flanks and crushed the two armies that were covering our advance, and that the Germans were almost about to encircle us.'

Nine days into the offensive, with the attack stalled, Vitman was ordered to report to the headquarters of the 6th Army about 6 kilometres from the front line, still within the threatened German encirclement: 'I saw there a lot of panic. They were packing headquarters documents in a great hurry.'

Almost immediately he arrived at headquarters Vitman was told to return to his regiment. On the road back to the front line he passed a convoy of Soviet soldiers going in the other direction. The officer in command told Vitman that his regiment had been cut off by the Germans and that he should join this unit, which was trying to break out. But as they retreated, they were caught in the open and shelled and bombed by the Germans. 'You could only hide in the old shell holes,' says Vitman. 'Actually I always preferred to lie not with my face down, but with my face up so I could see where the bombs were falling…. The earth was shaking. There was smoke going up, bits of bodies and uniforms flying into the air, and next to you there were bullets and splinters falling around. You don't think about anything. What can you think about? When I saw several bombs flying directly on me, I said to the soldier who was lying near me, "Let's run!" I managed to stand up and run away, but I was hit by the blast. Later, when I came back to see what had happened, all that was left of this other soldier was his bag and his gas mask.'

The Soviet troops became completely surrounded as the German flanks closed in on them. The panic intensified with each passing hour. Vitman watched as a commissar ripped the red star – the insignia that marked him as a political officer – from his sleeve and then, noticing there was a mark on his uniform showing where the star had been, began desperately rubbing mud over the fabric. When that failed he gave his tunic jacket away to a passing soldier and ran. Vitman saw another soldier throw down his rifle and say, 'For many years I was like a prisoner in a collective farm, and now it doesn't matter to me whether I live or not,' and then run to surrender.

Joachim Stempel fought on the German side at Kharkov. He remembers 'the astonished eyes of the Russians, who just couldn't believe what was going on here. They couldn't believe how much ground we had made up in the rearguard of their advance troops.' He describes the nights of the battle as 'unforgettable': 'The sight of thousands of Russians, who were trying to escape – a heaving mass of them – trying to reach freedom, shooting at us and being shot back at. Then, with a lot of shouting, trying to find gaps through which they could escape, and then being repulsed by the hail of bullets from our artillery and our guns…. The most horrifying pictures and impressions were the ones immediately after the attempted break-outs; awful, horrible wounds and many, many dead. I saw people with entire lower jaws just torn away, people with head wounds who were barely conscious but still driven on…. I had the impression that, at that point, it was every man for himself trying to find a way to get out of the cauldron.'

All around him Boris Vitman heard the moaning of the Soviet wounded, but no one was paying any attention to them. Nearby, in a dugout, the Red Army doctors and nurses lay completely drunk. 'I pointed my gun at them,' says Vitman, 'and said, "Come out and do something!" But they had got drunk because they could see that they wouldn't be able to help so many wounded.'

Vitman watched with horror as the Germans continued fighting. 'I thought they were real butchers because they were still firing when there were so many dead. And I realized that they couldn't take so many people prisoner, so they were trying to destroy as many of us as possible. German tanks began to approach, as well as armoured vehicles. At that moment our captain turned up. His head was bandaged and had blood on it. He shouted: "Attack!" About 20 people rose up, and I was one of them, even though my machine gun had no ammunition. We followed him, simply to die. Our group came under fire. People were falling down next to me and I kept thinking, well, when will my turn come? Then I saw an explosion, the earth went up, I lost consciousness for a moment, but quickly recovered and knew I was wounded in the leg.' Vitman looked up and saw a German armoured car about 20 metres away from him. Two soldiers with machine guns got down from the vehicle and walked towards him. '*Russ, komm, komm,*' they shouted. 'I found it difficult to stand because of my wound,' says Vitman. 'One ran towards me, whilst the other aimed his machine gun at my head. When they saw I really couldn't stand up they pulled me to my feet and threw me into the back of an open truck.'

Vitman was driven to a collection point for the wounded. The able-bodied were imprisoned nearby behind barbed wire and guarded by SS soldiers. He heard an announcement over a loudspeaker: 'Jews and commissars come forward!' The commissars were taken away, leaving about ten Jews behind. 'The Jews were given spades and told to dig a trench. It began to rain. After a while I could only see the tops of their heads. An SS man was hitting them to make them dig faster. When the trench was deep enough, he picked up a Russian machine gun and fired, shooting several salvos into the trench. We could hear them moaning. Then some more SS men turned up and finished them off. They were killed only because they were Jews. This had a shocking effect on me because then I saw what Nazism was. We were told that the Jews and commissars cannot have control over us any more, that the Germans had come to liberate us and soon we're going home. But I only knew I had to fight the Germans to the very end.'

Even though Boris Vitman had escaped immediate murder, since he was neither a commissar nor a Jew, he was still in great danger. A German doctor arrived and began a selection of the wounded – those still 'useful' to the Germans would be allowed to live for the moment, the rest left to die. Next to Vitman was a Soviet soldier who had been shot in the stomach. Knowing the importance of looking as though he had only a minor wound, he was trying to shove his intestines back inside his body. 'He looked so much at a loss,' says Vitman, 'and his eyes were asking: what shall I do with all this?'

Vitman himself was saved because he had learnt German at school and was able to act as a translator for the doctor. 'I noticed later that if a Russian could speak German then their attitude was quite different. When the man couldn't speak a foreign language the Germans thought it indicated that he was from an inferior race. But when they heard me speak German, they brought us water and didn't shoot us down.' Vitman was able to understand the conversations the Germans had amongst themselves, most notably when two senior SS men arrived in a headquarters car and stood nearby, looking at the mass of prisoners. 'I could hear one of them saying, "It's a shame Marshal Timoshenko is not present to see all this. The Führer has reserved a medal for him – the iron cross with oak leaves – to thank him for making such a big contribution to the German victory."'

Timoshenko had indeed made a large contribution to the German victory. Despite superiority in numbers, his attack had been crushed. By 28 May 1942 he had lost over a quarter of a million troops. The two Soviet armies caught around Barvenkovo (in what became known as the Barvenkovo 'mousetrap') were almost completely destroyed. 'It was a real disaster, a big disaster,' says Makhmud Gareev, a Red Army officer during the war who went on to the highest reaches of Soviet command in the post-war era. 'The failures of 1941 could be put down to the unexpected nature of the invasion and our unpreparedness, but in 1942, after we had carried out some defensive operations and after the front line had stabilized, all of a sudden such a major defeat.' And it was clear to soldiers like Gareev what one of the key reasons for this failure had been: 'It is linked to what happened in 1941 – to Stalin's incompetence, his lack of understanding of a strategic situation and his unwillingness to listen to others.'

'We [the German soldiers] were proud that we had managed to succeed so quickly,' says Joachim Stempel. 'I have to say that we all shared in the belief and the feeling that what we're doing will work. There's nothing we can't do, even if it's difficult and we're ill-equipped. We still believed and had faith that the leadership would provide, and then we'd make up the rest. And again, after the Kharkov cauldron [encirclement] where, once again, we were able to leave the battlefield victoriously, we were in high spirits and looked forward to what lay ahead.'

The German victory that soldiers like Stempel hoped for was not an impossibility in 1942. The Germans already held the agricultural heartland of the Soviet Union – the Ukraine – as well as the Donbas (Don River Basin) region, which had been the Soviets' main centre for coal and steel. With Stalin demonstrating at Kharkov that he appeared to have learnt nothing from the military disasters of the previous year, eventual Soviet defeat looked conceivable.

Hitler capitalized on the Soviet defeat

OVERLEAF Marshal Timoshenko (gesticulating) lectures Red Army soldiers before his disgrace at Kharkov. After the defeat he lost his operational command.

at Kharkov with his own ambitious Operation Blue – the plan to advance in the south towards Stalingrad, the mountains of the Caucasus and down to the Caspian Sea. This would deprive the Soviet war machine of access to its supply of oil and, Hitler believed, deal it a crushing economic blow from which it would not recover. The campaign's aim, he stated, was 'finally to annihilate what vital defensive strength the Soviets have left and to remove from their grasp as far as possible the principal sources of energy for their war economy'. A glance at the map shows how grandiose Operation Blue actually was – yet if Stalin had carried on leading the Red Army in such a foolhardy way, the German campaign could well have succeeded.

On 28 June 1942 the Germans attacked along virtually the whole southern front, with the 4th Panzer Army pushing on to Voronezh and the 1st Panzer Army advancing out from south of Kharkov. The Blitzkrieg moved swiftly, attempting as before to encircle whole Soviet armies, and initially as the Red Army fell back, the signs were that this might be a repeat of 1941. 'The main reason [for the German success] was that after we suffered defeat near Kharkov, a big gap appeared,' says Makhmud Gareev. 'The stability of the front had broken down. We didn't have any ready reserves. They had been used up for the offensives in different directions. Reserves had to be transferred from the Moscow direction, from the Leningrad direction, but the trouble was that these reserves were sent into combat immediately. Sending every new division into combat without proper preparation led to a worse and worse situation.'

At the end of July, after his troops had pushed on towards the River Don, Hitler decided to split his forces in two. Whilst Army Group A turned south to the oilfields of the Caucasus, the other spearhead, Army Group B, continued towards Stalingrad on the Volga. By this action Hitler demonstrated not just his impatience to accomplish several military objectives simultaneously but his own contempt once again for the Red Army.

Stalin watched the progress of Operation Blue and reacted with fury. He had preferred to believe that the German attack in the south was a mere diversionary thrust preparatory to the main attack on Moscow; now he searched for scapegoats amongst his intelligence officers. Then, as the Soviet forces fell further back, he issued his infamous order 227 – 'Not a step back' – which, amongst other harsh measures, confirmed the power of the 'backmarker' divisions to shoot any Soviet troops who tried to retreat without authorization, and formally introduced penal battalions to punish cowardice. Once again, at a moment of crisis, he believed the Red Army was best motivated by fear of terrible retribution if it failed.

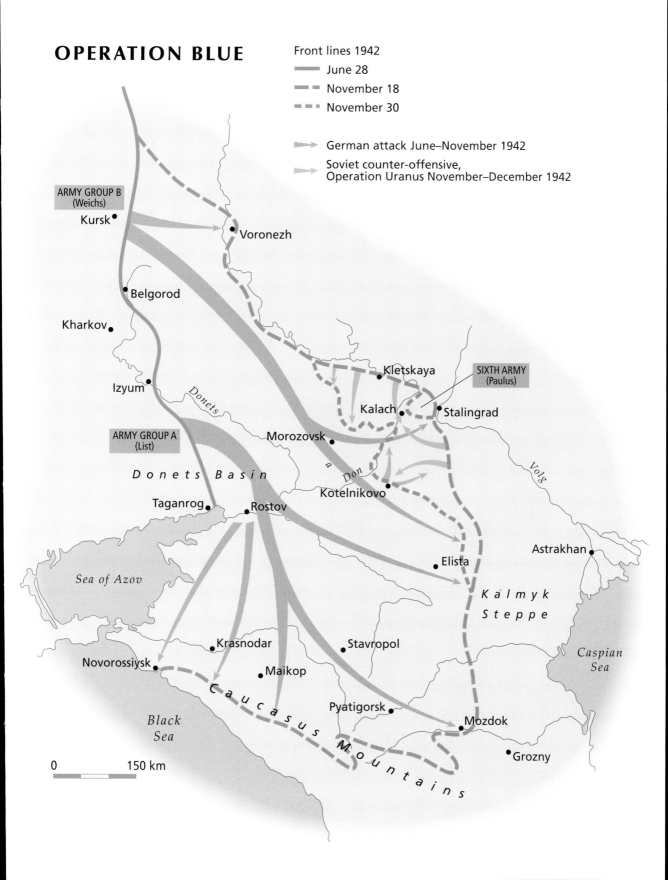

OPERATION BLUE

Front lines 1942
June 28
November 18
November 30

German attack June–November 1942

Soviet counter-offensive,
Operation Uranus November–December 1942

ARMY GROUP B
(Weichs)

Kursk

Voronezh

Belgorod

Kharkov

Izyum

Donets

ARMY GROUP A
(List)

Kletskaya

SIXTH ARMY
(Paulus)

Kalach

Stalingrad

Morozovsk

Don

Kotelnikovo

Donets Basin

Taganrog

Rostov

Volga

Astrakhan

Elista

Sea of Azov

*Kalmyk
Steppe*

Krasnodar

Stavropol

Caspian
Sea

Novorossiysk

Maikop

Caucasus

Pyatigorsk

Mozdok

Black
Sea

Grozny

Mountains

0   150 km

The brutality of Soviet discipline – particularly the personal experience of those who survived the penal battalions (*shtrafbaty*) – is an aspect of the war that the Communist Party historians preferred not to publicize. Only since the fall of Communism have men such as Vladimir Kantovski, who was sent to a penal battalion in 1942, felt free to tell their extraordinary true story.

Kantovski's troubles began in the spring of 1941 when, as an 18-year-old student in Moscow, he learnt that one of his teachers had been arrested. (Only recently has he been allowed access to the secret NKVD file that shows, ironically, that his teacher was imprisoned because he had been overheard voicing the view, just before the German invasion, that 'the Hitler/Stalin pact was dangerous for the safety of the Soviet Union'.)

So angry were Vladimir and his school friends at their teacher's arrest that they typed out a leaflet of protest and circulated it around the neighbourhood. They were all committed Communists and felt that the purity of their ideals had been sullied by this arbitrary oppression. 'We had our own understanding of Communism,' says Kantovski, 'and this honesty demanded that we act…. We didn't take Stalin and his henchmen seriously. But at the same time we remained patriots and in essence Communists. Although not Communists in the way Stalin understood it.'

Shortly after the war had begun, the NKVD came to Kantovski's flat and arrested him. By July he had been transferred to Omsk prison, east of Moscow, where he stayed for several months. 'You can write novels or poems about Omsk prison,' he says. 'Imagine a cell which has nine bunks. And there were between 50 and 60 of us in that room with nine beds and people were sleeping in the beds, under the beds, between the beds and in the gangway. We could leave the cell twice a day to go to the toilet and once a fortnight we were taken to the bath-house. But we were never allowed to walk in the courtyard and go out into the open air.'

For writing the pamphlet protesting at his teacher's arrest Kantovski was sentenced to ten years in a labour camp. But as soon as he was transferred from Omsk, he asked to be sent to the front line, since 'while the country was at war we felt guilty about sitting in prison'. To those in the West who want to believe that the undoubted brutality of the Soviet system was the sole reason the Red Army was capable of sacrificing so many of its soldiers in battle, Vladimir Kantovski's action will be inexplicable. For here is a man who *volunteered* to serve in one of Stalin's notorious penal battalions. What his story demonstrates is that the terror prevalent in the Soviet system is only part of the reason the Red Army fought as it did. In 1942 even prisoners unjustly held in the gulag could feel motivated to fight the Germans by their own patriotism and belief in the Communist ideal.

After Stalin issued order 227 in the summer of 1942, Kantovski learnt that his request had been granted; he would be sent to the front line, his sentence commuted from ten years to five. He became one of the 440,000 Soviet soldiers who served in penal battalions; how many survived the war is not known for sure, but it is likely to be the merest handful.

OPPOSITE Soviet resistance in August 1942. By now the Red Army had learnt the art of defensive retreat. To Hitler's dismay, the days of massive encirclements of Soviet armies were over.

OVERLEAF A German tank crosses a pontoon bridge during their advance south-east in Operation Blue during the summer of 1942. The wide, flat steppes enabled German motorized units to make swift progress.

Once at the front line he met the other members of his battalion: 'I was the only one who was convicted on political charges – usually the penal battalions were made up of people who had committed various minor crimes like being late for work, which was a crime at that time. If you were more than 21 minutes late, it meant a year in prison, but instead of that you could go to a penal battalion. Or a small theft or if you were rude to someone in the street – that could all be considered a crime and you could be sent to a penal battalion.'

Kantovski knew that in a penal battalion 'my old sins could only be pardoned through my blood' – and that the only realistic chance he had of survival was to be wounded in combat. Yet he 'never regretted for a single minute' that he chose to join one: 'It's my nature. I don't like to muse over decisions I've taken – I never do it on principle. And in spite of everything, some opportunities were opening up for me. There was a small chance of survival – even if 10 people survived out of 250 it meant that you had a chance.'

After receiving 'no training whatsoever', Kantovski's unit was marched to the front line and told they would have the opportunity of serving the Motherland by 'reconnaissance through combat'. They were required to advance towards the German lines and 'make the enemy's weapons fire so that our reconnaissance people could spot the sources of the enemy's fire and later destroy them'. They were ordered forward at dawn towards a wood occupied by Germans about 400 metres from the Soviet positions. 'As soon as we showed ourselves, the enemy opened fire. And our officers shouted, "Onwards, onwards!" I don't think you can feel any patriotism when you are participating in such an attack. I think the over-riding feeling is one of bluntness – your feelings are blunted. You feel fatalistic. You know what's happening is unavoidable, fatal, and it's like a game of Russian roulette. Well, what is your lot going to be?'

As the penal battalion advanced, the German machine gun fire intensified. The four or five Soviet tanks that accompanied them were swiftly destroyed. Then Kantovski felt bullets hit his arm and shoulder: 'I was wounded and I began to bleed. You had to be heavily wounded to be pardoned, but how can you know whether you are badly wounded or not badly wounded? Until I became convinced that I was heavily enough wounded I didn't dare set off towards the first aid centre. It was very hard to move – my arm was not working, so I had to crawl lying on my back.'

Out of his unit of 240, only nine escaped being severely wounded or killed. Luckily for Kantovski, his wound was considered serious enough for him to be medically treated and released from the penal battalion. He then returned to Moscow where he was able to continue as a student. But his story does not end there. In 1944 he was arrested again and charged with the same offence he had committed in 1941. His NKVD investigator just told him, 'In 1941 you were sentenced to ten years. All right, go back and do your time and you'll finish in 1951.' Kantovski never knew why he had been sent back to the gulag. 'We lived under Stalin's personal dictatorship,' he says. 'I didn't query whether Stalin was just or unjust – he was simply a tyrant. All of it rested on fear, on cruelty, on informing – on sticks without any carrots.'

In the course of making the television series on which this book is based some truly exceptional people emerged. But Vladimir Kantovski was one of the most impressive. Sitting in his small Moscow flat, he unravelled a personal story that was rife with injustice at every turn. Yet all his personal misfortune – even the wounds whose scars he still bears today from his experience of 'reconnaissance through combat' – stemmed from writing that pamphlet of protest in 1941 about the arrest of his teacher. It was hard to see what that pamphlet had achieved apart from his own suffering. Looking back, didn't he regret ever having written it? 'I don't regret having done it,' he replied. 'Because not everyone could say at the time that he had the liberty to express himself. My personality grew stronger.' He paused for a moment, trying to find the exact words that would convey his feeling. Then he finally said, 'I don't regret it because it gives me self-respect.' In a war that is rich in stories of suffering which have no redemption, it is worth remembering the personal experience of Vladimir Kantovski – a man who was prepared to die not just for his country, but for his own sense of self-worth.

Yet no amount of personal sacrifice seemed able to stem the advance of the Germans in the summer of 1942. On 23 July Panzer divisions advanced into Rostov as far as the bridge across the River Don. 'The Germans were so confident,' says Anatoly Mereshko, a Soviet officer who fought against them that summer, 'which was natural because they moved from Kharkov to the Don…. It would make anyone confident. They walked, having rolled up their sleeves, wearing shorts and singing their songs. As for our retreating units, they were really completely demoralized people. They didn't know where they were going and they didn't know where to look for their units. For example, they were told to reassemble in Marinovka, but where was Marinovka? About five or six soldiers would turn up and ask: "Where is Marinovka?" So they just walked and walked, carrying their weapons with them – because without weapons they would be interrogated.'

Tamara Kalmykova, then an 18-year-old student, witnessed the Soviet retreat: 'There was terrible panic – each was frightened for his life. And I used to say that if I had a

Panzer units advanced further and further into the vast steppes. It was an exhilarating and sometimes bewildering experience for these men – more like crossing an ocean than land. ABOVE A German shell hits a Russian house. BELOW Panzer unit in the Kalmyk steppe.

machine gun I would have killed all those who were retreating. Because every step of the retreat doubled the amount of blood that needed to be shed – afterwards you will need two or three times the casualties to win it back.'

Stalin must have felt similar sentiments – that was why he issued his order: 'Not one step back.' But that summer he also accepted that on occasion it would be necessary to conduct staged withdrawals to prevent his forces being encircled. It was a breakthrough – the first significant sign that he was prepared to learn from his earlier mistakes and listen to the generals around him. Only by a fighting retreat could similar disasters to Kharkov that spring and to Kiev and Vyazma the previous year be avoided.

That summer Anatoly Mereshko commanded an élite unit of officer cadets in the fight against Operation Blue. For him and his unit, each day had the same essential pattern. 'Usually the Germans attacked twice and then waited for the main forces to pull up for a larger attack the next morning. When the evening came, all warfare stopped. But they sent their motorcyclists to the flanks where they fired light rockets – they just did it to give the impression of encirclement. The Germans did everything according to schedule. At dawn their reconnaissance plane usually arrived. Then the bombers came. They bombed the front line, and then the shelling began, and then infantry and tanks attacked. If you could withstand the bombing and the shelling, it was fine because you could always fight back against the tanks and the infantry. If they had no success, they stopped their attacks.' During the night, whilst the Germans called up more reinforcements, the Red Army melted away. 'We had no strength to hold the defence,' says Mereshko. 'If we had been given the order to hold out and stay, we would have stayed, but the command preferred to save us.' Ironically, these new pragmatic tactics did not please either him or his men: 'We felt desperation and anger because of our helplessness, and we also wondered: "Why do they not let us properly fight the enemy? Why do we have to keep on withdrawing?" And we kept withdrawing, as far as the River Don.'

'Our initial impression was that the Russians were fleeing,' says Joachim Stempel who, as a German tank officer, fought his way across the steppes in Operation Blue. 'But that turned out to be a mistake.' The Red Army was, of course, making a strategic retreat – though to many of the soldiers on the ground the impression must have been that this was a repeat of 1941. But this time there were no great German encirclements, and the hit-and-run Soviet defensive tactics sapped the strength of the German advance. 'If we caught up with the Russians during the day,' says Gerhard Münch, who fought in Army Group B, 'then during the night they'd go further away from us. This is the time when I first heard the term "The Russians fighting by space", which means he lets us enter and our difficulties with supply get bigger and the ways of supply get more complicated.' Münch's regimental commander expressed similar doubts to him during the advance to Stalingrad. 'He was very sceptical after Kharkov because he said, "This huge space – what on earth are we supposed to do here?" And when we were not able to get at the enemy, he made the point that our opponent was using space against us.'

That summer the Red Army was careful about choosing the moment to mount a defence against the Germans and the moment to withdraw. Bridgeheads and other important strategic positions would be held and fiercely defended until the threat of encirclement became too great. Joachim Stempel and his men saw at first-hand this new sophistication in Red Army tactics once they crossed the River Don and encountered a Soviet defensive obstacle the like of which they had not seen before. 'Here we experienced incredibly heavy losses,' he says. 'Behind every little hill, every little rise, there were built-in T.34 tanks. Only the gun barrels were visible, and we were really surprised when they opened fire – we hadn't really recognized them. And particularly terrible were the Russian flame-thrower divisions, who, at temperatures of 40 degrees, just lit up everything that was at all flammable and we had the most terrible injuries and burns…. And the closer we got to Stalingrad, the harder was the resistance of the Soviet troops.'

Hitler was determined that Stalingrad should be taken. The city was an important industrial centre and dominated the Volga, the river along which the Soviets moved vital supplies up from the Caucasus. If Moscow and the other northern cities could be cut off from this southern oil, the Soviets would be struck a devastating economic blow. (Hitler's intense interest may also have been fuelled by the city's very name – Stalingrad had been renamed in honour of the Soviet leader after his alleged exploits there during the civil war.)

The 4th Panzer Army, together with the 6th Army, converged on the city, which lay spread out in front of them like a ribbon for 50 kilometres or so along the Volga. A more difficult city to defend could scarcely be imagined. The river formed a natural barrier, and once the Germans surrounded the city on the remaining three sides, all reinforcements would have to make the dangerous journey across the water.

On Sunday, 23 August the Germans launched a 600-bomber raid on Stalingrad – the most intense aerial bombardment so far seen on the Eastern Front. That morning Valentina Krutova, an 11-year-old schoolgirl, and her 14-year-old brother Yuri were picking berries on the city outskirts when they heard the sound of a massive armada of planes. As they looked up, the bombs began to fall. 'Everything was ablaze,' she says. 'There was screaming…. While an adult could have been able to understand that there was a war going on, what could we understand, being children? We were only scared that we would be killed.'

'When the bombing began, it was really horrible,' says Albert Burkovski, who was 14 in 1942. 'I can still remember the planes, the noise they were making, and it became real hell. I don't know how people managed to bear it. It was all one big fire. We climbed to the roof and we could hear the moaning, groaning from down below.' Once the bombing had stopped, Albert ran back home towards the house he lived in with his grandmother. When he turned on to their street, he saw that his house had become a pile of rubble. 'Once we came back there was only moaning and more moaning coming from under the ruins. My grandmother had been hiding in the basement of the house, but it was all closed in by the ruins – everyone in there was crushed. I thought for some time that I had better be killed because such was my grief, my misery, because I was all alone.'

Stalin resolved to hold the city. The Red Army had retreated hundreds of kilometres from Kharkov in the Ukraine, and a stand had to be made on the Volga. Initially he refused to allow even the civilian population to escape across the river. There would be no more running away. Here the Red Army would stay and fight.

At his new headquarters at Vinnitsa in the Ukraine, Hitler sweated in the fierce summer heat. Despite the progress that had been made by both Army Groups, no Soviet armies had been encircled. Fanning Hitler's annoyance, General Halder, the Chief of the Army General Staff, suggested that there might not be enough resources available to support both Army Groups and enable them to meet their objectives simultaneously. Hitler was furious. Halder recorded in his war diary on 30 August: 'Today's conference with the Führer was again an occasion for abusive reproaches against the military leadership abilities of the highest commanders. He charges them with intellectual conceit, mental inadaptability, and utter failure to grasp the essentials.'

At the beginning of September there was another row as Field Marshal List's Army Group A, fighting in the Caucasus, appeared to slow in its advance. Jodl, Chief of the Operations Staff of the High Command of the Armed

OVERLEAF A meeting at Hitler's headquarters in East Prussia. Leaning on the map table (left to right) are Field Marshal Manstein, who made the doomed attempt to relieve the 6th Army in Stalingrad, Hitler and General Kurt Zeitzler, who replaced Halder as Chief of the General Staff in September 1942.

Forces, supported List's actions, saying that he was following previous instructions from the Führer. Hitler was beside himself with anger. List was removed and on 9 September Hitler personally took command of Army Group A, which was advancing across the steppes about 1600 kilometres away. This led to a bizarre command structure in which, as commander of an army group, Hitler was answerable to himself as Commander-in-Chief of the Army, then to himself again as Supreme Commander-in-Chief of the Wehrmacht (all the German Armed forces), and finally to himself again as Head of State. Then, as if the atmosphere of change was not fetid enough, on 22 September Hitler replaced Halder as Chief of Staff with Kurt Zeitzler, a general famed for his obsequiousness. So, at the same time as Stalin was learning to listen to the advice of those around him, Hitler was creating an impractical military structure which crushed individual initiative and in which his military commanders knew what fate to expect if they dared criticize their all-knowing Führer.

Meanwhile, after the bombing of Stalingrad, in the last week of August the Germans finally reached the Volga. By 3 September the city was surrounded. 'We came to a rise which offered a very good view of Stalingrad,' says Joachim Stempel. 'The city was in flames and suddenly, like a silver ribbon, I saw the Volga. It came as quite a surprise. We all knew we had to get there – that's our goal, maybe the goal of the whole war…. It was a very impressive thing to be standing on the border with Asia and being able to say – we're at the Volga! In spite of all the casualties, all the hardships, we had managed to attain this goal, this victory. The Volga! It was within our grasp! The Volga was a very impressive sight in the autumn sun. A river of a width which we don't know in Germany. And this incredible view into the depths of Asia – nothing but forests, more forests, plains and the endless horizon. It was an inspirational feeling for anyone who had been involved in breaking through the Russian defences, the taking of ground, the loss of good comrades who couldn't experience this with us. And now before us, this picture, the Volga, close enough to touch. We thought, it can't take much longer now – we're here.'

As the Germans moved forward into the city, thousands of civilians became trapped behind their lines. Valentina Krutova, together with her brother Yuri and five-year-old sister, were amongst those cut off from the

narrowing Soviet-held section of the city. They lived with their grandmother, who was badly wounded as the result of an explosion. 'Germans often came into our house,' says Valentina. 'They would open the door and look in. But as our granny was really rotting alive and the Germans were very much afraid of various diseases, they didn't come very close. The Germans saw there were blisters on her body and little worms had appeared in her wounds. It smelt terrible.'

A Red Army supply boat sinks while crossing the Volga to reinforce Stalingrad in autumn 1942. German fire made daylight crossing deadly, and these Soviet soldiers, weighed down with equipment, would have quickly drowned.

ABOVE AND BELOW Two photographs taken as Army Group A invaded the mountains of the Caucasus. After crossing the steppes and climbing these mountains, it must have seemed to many of these German soldiers that they were advancing to the end of the world.

There was no medical care available, and shortly after the Germans arrived her grandmother died. 'When she died we carried her, we actually pulled her body on some piece of cloth into a trench and put the piece of cloth on her to protect her face from the earth, and then we buried her. We couldn't find the place afterwards. It was very hard for us because we used to feel some support from her when she was alive. Although she was bedridden, she was with us, she was a living human being. We could talk to her. She would hug us and express her sympathy and this warmed our hearts. We didn't feel too burdened by fear, although we were living on the territory occupied by the Germans. But when we lost her, it began to be emotionally very difficult for us. We had no one else to support us.'

Three children on their own amongst the thousands trapped in Stalingrad had little chance of survival, but 14-year-old Yuri did what he could to scavenge food. 'My brother used to go to a grain elevator where a small amount of grain remained, and he gave us a little bit every day and it helped us. He kept the bag between the window panes. One day a German officer and two soldiers – they were either Germans or Romanians – came in and began demanding food. They wanted eggs and chicken and bread. And we had nothing. They began to search for food, and were clever enough to look between the window panes and they found that little bag with wheat. They wanted to shoot us down. My brother and I went down on our knees and pleaded with them not to kill us. The German officer was young. He began to say something to his soldiers. They took away the grain but they left us alone.'

Albert Burkovski was another child left on his own in the city, but he was lucky – he was on the Soviet side of the divide. In the first days of the bombardment he and a school friend helped transport wounded

Albert Burkovski as a boy soldier 'adopted' by the Soviet 13th Division in Stalingrad. OVERLEAF Children huddle in the ruins of Stalingrad. Thousands of young children were left orphaned by the fighting and, like Valentina Krutova, struggled to survive as best they could.

Red Army soldiers down to the landing stage on the Volga by pushing them in a cart. 'We brought the wounded to the river crossing and could see cutters and boats and rafts approaching. The Germans were firing, and the firing was heavy.' Many of the Soviet boats were destroyed before they reached the bank. 'The crossing was terrible. There was so much shelling and bombing that, even if you could swim – well, you could get killed.'

Hitler had ordered that Stalingrad be taken, but Stalin had commanded that it be held. This city, which at the start of Operation Blue had been seen as merely one target amongst many, had unexpectedly become the operation's main objective – almost the focal point of the whole war. Stalin ordered the Red Army to retain the Stalingrad bank of the Volga, using whatever means were necessary.

In such brutal circumstances the character of the two commanders in the battle was to prove crucial. Leading the German 6th Army was the sophisticated Friedrich Paulus, an experienced staff officer who had previously served as deputy Chief of Staff under General Halder. 'Paulus was very tall and he was very calm and poised,' says Günther von Below, who served under him in the 6th Army. 'He was a very wise man with a very humane attitude. He was always somewhat hesitant in his decisions – one had to help him decide.... On one occasion I said to him, "General, if you don't sign here and now, I will sign on your behalf this very instant." And then he signed the paper. And he laughed and said: "So much for that."'

ABOVE Friedrich Paulus, commander of the German 6th Army.
OPPOSITE Vasily Chuikov, commander of the Soviet 62nd Army at Stalingrad.

In command of the Soviet 62nd Army at Stalingrad, from September 1942 onwards, was a very different man – Vasily Chuikov. If Paulus was a strategist, aware of the grand sweep of war, then Chuikov was a tactician, focused on the struggle to take an individual street or building. If Paulus was courteous, almost deferential, then Chuikov was a bully whose brutal treatment of those he believed had failed him was legendary.

'Chuikov could sense the nature of a battle,' says Anatoly Mereshko, who served with him at Stalingrad. 'And he could take timely decisions in spite of all obstacles to carry out that decision. He had persistence and perseverance.... Chuikov combined the Russian features, which are, as one song puts it, "If you shoot, you shoot; if you make merry, you make merry," and for Chuikov shooting came first. He had colossal energy that was very catching, and it passed on to more junior commanders and then on to soldiers. If Chuikov's character had been different, then we wouldn't have held Stalingrad.'

A crucial part of Chuikov's character was his brutality. If a commander acted in a way he disliked, Chuikov would physically assault him: 'He went as far as beating people with his fists or with a stick,' says Mereshko, 'for which Stalin told him off. He used to lean on a stick, and if he didn't like the behaviour of a particular commander, he could hit this commander with his stick on his back.' Later in the war Mereshko had personal experience of this side of Chuikov: 'I went into the house where the operational department was, and I could see my boss leaning against the wall with the table overturned. He was holding a handkerchief to his nose and there was blood on it. He said to me that Chuikov had hit him.' Mereshko's superior officer explained the simple reason he had been assaulted by Chuikov: 'The General Colonel had hit the Lieutenant Colonel because he was dissatisfied with the report he had received.' Then his boss added, 'Well, it's good that you've just come, not one minute before, because otherwise he would have hit you too.'

Chuikov was one of a new breed of Soviet commander, not one of Stalin's creatures picked primarily for his subservience but a ruthless and competent leader. He knew that he was required to hold Stalingrad or die in the attempt. He also knew that he had to impose the harshest discipline imaginable on the troops he commanded in order to achieve his aim; more than 13,000 of them were arrested – and many of that number executed – during the Battle of Stalingrad. Yet again, the Soviet system sought to fight 'fear with fear', as the Red Army was told retreat was impossible and that 'there is no land beyond the Volga'.

The shrewd tactician in Chuikov also realized that the ruined city allowed the Red Army, for the first time in the conflict, to fight a different kind of war – one in which individual bravery and resilience would count as much as high-flown strategy. The Soviet troops would inhabit the city like 'living concrete' and take on the Germans in hand-to-hand fighting. Chuikov decreed that the Soviet troops must station themselves as close as possible to the German front line. That way the German bombers and artillery risked hitting their own men in any attack. The motto of the Soviet defenders became, 'Don't get far from the enemy.' 'Our principle was, we'll put claws in the throat of the enemy and hold them very close,' says Anatoly Mereshko. 'That way you can stay alive. These were Chuikov's tactics. The gap between you and the enemy should not be bigger than 50 or 100 metres, or not more than a grenade's throw. If we threw a grenade, we had only four seconds before the explosion happened. When the Germans threw their grenades, they fell into our trenches and our soldiers could lift the grenade up and throw it back because the German grenades exploded

The consequences of five months of bitter fighting – an aerial picture of Stalingrad taken after the battle in 1943.

after nine or ten seconds. So we took advantage of the weakness of the German grenades. That was also due to Chuikov.'

Chuikov also perfected the use of assault groups to clear German-held houses. 'Such a group could vary between five and 50 people, without their rucksacks, only with grenades, and their job was to rush into the house,' says Mereshko. 'And then this assault group would be followed by a consolidation group. The assault group had to send the Germans into panic, but the consolidation group that followed had to repel the Germans' counter-attack.'

These house clearances were the stuff of nightmares. Suren Mirzoyan is one of the few survivors of these operations from the Soviet side, and described a typical assault group encounter with the Germans: 'Only the outer wall of the house survived, but inside there was rubble and the Germans had hidden amongst it. Suddenly one German jumped on my friend and he reacted and hit the German with his knee. And then a second German jumped on him and I lashed out against him – we had knives. Do you know when you press a ripe tomato, juice comes out? I stabbed him with a knife and everything around was in blood. I felt only one thing – kill, kill. A beast. And another German jumped on me and he was shouting and then he fell. If you were not strong enough physically, the German would have swallowed you. Each metre of Stalingrad meant possible death. Death was in our pockets. Death was always on our steps.'

During these primitive encounters Mirzoyan preferred not to use modern weaponry: 'I tried not to use [these] weapons against people. I had a knife or a spade – a very sharp spade. It's better than a machine gun sometimes. I also used the spade in the front lines. You dig with your spade and then you can use it in man-to-man fighting. A machine gun takes a long time – you have to load it. But with a spade you simply lift it and you strike. It makes sense. These spades were very crucial in fighting.'

In the middle of September the Germans mounted a determined attack and managed to reach Stalingrad's central railway station. Supported by the 13th Guards Division, Chuikov and his men fought back. Chuikov's own determination to cling to the river bank or die in the attempt became an inspiration to his men. Every factory, every street, every house became a battlefield.

The savagery of the fighting amongst the rubble of Stalingrad was the antithesis of Blitzkrieg. This was not sophisticated combat but primitive struggle, as Helmut Walz, a private in the German 305th Infantry Division, discovered to his cost on the morning of 17 October when he and his unit were in the ruins of a factory: 'We had the order to advance, in the open space, to the factory buildings. It was a desert of rubble. Everything was mixed up together.' About 15 metres in front of him he saw Soviet soldiers in a dugout: 'I advanced about 10 metres, so that I was roughly 5 or 6 metres away from them, and hid behind a heap of concrete. I called out to them in Russian to surrender, but they didn't. Everywhere it was burning – bullets were flying through the air – so I threw a hand grenade right into the middle of them. And then one of them came out with blood running from his nose, his ears and his mouth. I don't know anything about medicine but when I saw him I knew that he wouldn't be able to survive – something inside his body was torn. And he aimed his machine gun at me – the Russian machine gun with the little drum at the front – and I said to myself, "Boy, you ain't going to get me!" And I aimed my gun at him. And then I saw little stars shooting out of the air. For a moment I was numb. What's going on? I ran my left hand over my face and a jet of blood came out and my teeth flew out of my mouth.'

One of Walz's comrades, seeing what had happened, leapt up on to a mass of concrete and then crashed down hard on top of the Soviet soldier. 'He jumped straight into the face of that Russian with his boots,' says Walz. 'I can still hear the face cracking – he kicked him to death, probably.' Walz's lieutenant gestured to him to move into the protection of a bomb crater where the officer bandaged Walz as best he could, but then another Red Army soldier appeared above them. 'The Russian aimed his machine gun at him [the lieutenant] and then his steel helmet flew off – it was a bull's-eye shot, right into his head,' says Walz. 'His head was open and I could see his brain, on the right, left and in the middle – there was water but no blood. He looked at me and then he fell into the rim of the crater.' Another German killed the Red Army soldier who had shot the lieutenant, and Walz crawled away to search for a medic.

By the end of that one day in October, out of a total of 77 soldiers in his company 'nobody was left – they were all either dead or wounded. The whole company had gone.'

The very proximity of the enemy in Stalingrad also led to bizarre, almost friendly, encounters. 'Imagine us in house-to-house fighting,' says Anatoly Mereshko. 'We took the third floor and the Germans took the first and second floors. By midday both sides get tired and the Germans shout, "Hi, Russians!" "What do you want, Germans?" we'd say. "Can you send us some water?" they'd answer. And we'd shout, "Let's swap pots filled with water for a pot filled with cigarettes." And then one hour later we'd carry on, we'd open fire again. Or the Germans cry, "Well, we have no cigarettes. We can send you a couple of clocks or watches." Well, then we swapped water for cigarettes or water for

vodka or for schnapps, and we honestly stopped fighting during that hour of swapping. Eventually either they kicked us out of the house or we kicked them out – it was proper fighting, the strongest side winning.'

This was a form of warfare for which the Germans had not been prepared. 'Hand-to-hand combat, positional warfare,' says Joachim Stempel, 'I don't want to say it was entirely foreign, but they were elements of our training which were very much on the fringe. We were an offensive army, trained for attack, and we were able to defend ourselves, of course, but we didn't have the experience of the Russian soldiers, whose training, whose nature and whose psyche of being tied to his native soil were all thrown into the mix. We didn't have that, and I think that we had more casualties because we weren't as close to nature as the Russians…. The Russians had the advantage in trench warfare and hand-to-hand combat – there's no doubt. As a tank unit, we were used to driving tanks and trying to bring the enemy down with tanks and then stopping, clearing the area and moving forward. But that was all forgotten in the past, a long time ago.'

The frustration for the Germans was intense, for the Volga was so close. 'Again and again, we heard, "Another hundred metres and you're there!" But how can you do it if you just don't have the strength left? It wasn't attacking as we were used to attacking. Here we remained in position for weeks and tried hard to win some land, even if it's only 10 or 15 metres which we managed to take from the Russians – that was considered a success. But the main thing was that the Russians were defending a narrow strip of land, maybe 300 metres deep, on the steep slopes down to the Volga where the command headquarters of the Russian armies and divisions were located. And the soldiers who were on duty there were completely fanatical about it, and obsessed with their mission. "You have to hold this because your generals are behind you!" And that made it impossible for us to take those last hundred metres, which was our constant aim.'

Gerhard Münch, by now a battalion commander, quickly realized that with the available resources house-to-house combat could not be won by either side: 'If the enemy has the stairwell or is on the first floor, then you don't even need to try [to take the house] because you just won't succeed. Once you get a demonstration of how unsuccessful any attempt to get into another building is, and if you're lucky enough to get back the injured people, then you just stop trying it. And so, in this section, the whole battle came to a standstill…it was not possible to change anything – unless you

OPPOSITE Red Army soldiers make the best use of available cover in the rubble of Stalingrad. The sophisticated techniques of armoured warfare were useless against these men.

got five new divisions that came in, but I think they probably would not have been able to do anything either.'

Throughout the city, the German advance bogged down. The Soviet snipers who hid in the rubble of the city made any movement from cover during daylight potentially fatal. These snipers were feared and detested. They became symbolic of the dishonourable, degrading and primitive way in which many Germans believed the Battle of Stalingrad was being fought. 'The Russian sniper who worked in our sector is again and again celebrated as a major hero,' says Gerhard Münch. 'I found it inwardly revolting. I always compared it with sitting in a raised hide and shooting deer – that's got nothing to do with soldiership in my personal opinion.'

'It became increasingly more difficult,' says Joachim Stempel, 'because every attack cost us so many casualties that it was possible to work out that, soon, there won't be anyone left. And we knew that the Russians at night were taking people across the Volga, but we had nothing left and so we had to keep going, nailed to the spot.' The German side received reinforcements too – but inexperience could prove swiftly fatal in the ruins of Stalingrad: 'I can remember something that was unforgettable, a cry of joy from the battalion, when we heard: "Tonight you'll get 60 or 70 men from the reserves." And, of course, that was such a message of hope that it just made you forget about everything else. And then, when they arrived, these boys, all about 18 or 19 years old, had had about four weeks' training. But that night, all hell broke loose. First, there was Russian artillery fire, then a Russian night offensive into our trenches. And with great difficulty – in fact, the commander of the battalion personally came down to the front to help me – we managed to push the Russians back out of the trenches. We lost more than half of these boys, dead or wounded, and they'd only just arrived. And the reason for that was because they lacked that sense, that instinct for danger, crisis, that you need in such situations – they just couldn't react like the old hands were able to react.'

Some of the fiercest fighting was for the Mamaev Kurgan, the ancient burial mound on the edge of the city. Whoever held this hill commanded a clear view of the centre of Stalingrad and the Volga just beyond. This key strategic point changed hands many times during the battle, sometimes several times in one day. Albert Burkovski took part in the fight. He had been 'adopted' by the Soviet 13th Guards Rifle Division, and at 14 became one of the youngest soldiers to fight in the defence of Stalingrad. 'I remember walking on the dead, decomposing bodies on the Mamaev Kurgan,' he says. 'Imagine, I put my foot on the ground and when I lift it I see that it's all dirty with somebody's intestines. It will never get erased from my memory…. But the most horrible experience was when I killed the first German. The Germans made about 15 or 20 attacks [on the Mamaev Kurgan] during the day. First came the bombing, then the artillery fire, then tanks went ahead and then the infantry. And all of a sudden I saw this German standing and looking away from me. He didn't see me because I was all covered with dust and earth. When I saw that huge German, I immediately fired at him without standing up. When you shoot at short range, then bits of the body immediately go up. I could see bits of him and I could smell the smell of his clothes because it was very close. And my comrades began to calm me down…I was vomiting. Other men were saying to me, "Come on, this is just a German," but none the less I was shivering all over. And it stayed in my memory forever.'

To escape German bombardment the Soviet defenders dug a series of underground hideouts in the bank of the Volga. Chuikov's headquarters were built deep in the earth only a few

Chuikov's headquarters at Stalingrad, dug deep into the Volga river bank.

metres from the river. 'If you wanted to live, you had to dig trenches and shelters,' says Burkovski. 'There were a lot of lice because there was no time to take a wash. But no one fell ill because our nerves were so much on edge that they didn't let us become sick.' A short distance along the river another Soviet commander lived in a sewer and held command meetings on planks just above the running water. The Germans had not witnessed this level of determination from the Red Army before. 'I think only Russians can get used to such hardships,' says Anatoly Mereshko phlegmatically.

Women soldiers – as pilots, communications officers and more – served throughout the Soviet forces.

And it wasn't just Soviet men who were fighting to defend Stalingrad. Relatively little attention has been given in the West to the vital contribution that female soldiers made to the fighting strength of the Red Army – at least 800,000 women served in Soviet forces during the war. Tamara Kalmykova, who became a

communications officer that summer with the 64th Army, was one of the thousands of female soldiers who helped defend Stalingrad. 'When we reached the Stalingrad front,' she says, 'we learnt we had to rely on ourselves and set right all the mistakes that were made in the first years of the war.... Women were more enduring, although they are the weaker sex. As Chuikov put it, "You can trust something to a woman. You feel confident that your order will be fulfilled at any cost." Because a woman is a mother who gives birth. Any mother is going to stand firm to protect her children the same way animals defend their cubs.... And women were merciless. They were avenging their husbands or brothers – in the families of practically all the women who were fighting, somebody had died. And nothing remained of their homes but ashes. Anyone, from any country, would want to take revenge. And this is what called them to action and gave them the strength and patience and courage to fulfil such a difficult job.'

Even though she was classed as a communications officer, Kalmykova also took part in the savage fighting just outside the city: 'During the battle, when we were walking along the communications channel, there was a cry that a gunner had been killed. I ran and my friend, a nurse, ran after me. She began to bandage him but he was dead. So she lay down next to the machine gun and started firing and I helped her, giving her the cartridges, and we managed to repel the German attack. But she was killed. I felt such anger against the enemy for killing my friend...and I was so sorry for her. She was only 18. She hadn't seen anything in life.'

Shortly afterwards Tamara Kalmykova was able to take her revenge on the Germans – but at great personal risk. The communications cable laid to the neighbouring battalion had been cut and her commander had sent two soldiers – a man and a woman – ahead to follow the wire and repair the damage. But neither of them had returned. So he ordered Kalmykova to find out what had happened to them. 'I followed the cable for 3 kilometres,' she says. 'And then I saw our young man – killed. He was lying dead, shot in the head. I went on following the cable and saw the girl. She was also dead, shot in the back of her head and in her spine. I picked up the documents of each of them and went on to look for the break in the cable so that I could repair it.'

'Suddenly I noticed a German in the bushes. I thought it was my end. I began to crawl back, but the heavy rifle that I had made it difficult. But the German had a sub-machine gun. It was easy for him to fire his sub-machine gun and to kill me, but he wanted to take me alive as a prisoner for interrogation because he saw I was a communications officer and knew a lot. But I managed to shoot at him. He fell down. At first I didn't believe he was really dead because I thought he was playing a trick and that he wanted me to go towards him. When I was sure he was really dead, I approached him. I didn't look at his face. I just put my hands into his pockets to get his documents. I felt a real repulsion when I was picking things from his pockets. But if I hadn't brought his documents back, they wouldn't have believed that I had killed him. When I returned, my commander was surprised to see me with a German backpack and a machine gun. I fell on my bunk bed and felt very weak. It was very frightening. But nevertheless I had to do what I had done – because if I hadn't I would have been killed. If you stayed idle, then you would surely die. Either you act against him or he acts against you. The logic is clear.'

Determined Soviet resistance had meant that the initial German thrust into the heart of the city had been held in September. By October, despite more fierce German attacks, the Red Army still held a strip of land in front of the Volga. Hitler was impatient. The 6th Army contained more than 300,000 men – why couldn't they take one ruined town? But the problem, as the German veterans of Stalingrad still emphasize today, was that even Paulus did not have enough men at his disposal to be sure of eliminating the Red Army soldiers who hid in the buildings and the sewers. The Volga, which the Germans had initially believed acted to their advantage in that it prevented the Soviets' retreat and made reinforcement hazardous, now became a hindrance since it prevented the 6th Army completely encircling their enemy.

Whilst the Germans wrestled with the unexpected difficulties that this new situation presented, Stalin and his generals debated how they should respond. Gradually, since the débâcle at Kharkov in May, Stalin had become less dogmatic in his military thinking. Now junior commanders were taught the German tactics of Blitzkrieg. 'I have to admit that we learnt to fight from the Germans,' says Tamara Kalmykova. 'Specifically, in coordination of troops, reconnaissance, communications and cartography.'

A key part of the learning process was to build on the practice of sending snatch squads across the German lines to capture prisoners for interrogation. These missions were dangerous in the extreme. Suren Mirzoyan was selected with one of his comrades for just such a task in the summer of 1942. They crept across no man's land until they encountered the enemy: 'We found out in what buildings the Germans were and then we crawled through the potato fields, we crawled and crawled and crawled until we got near one German guard. He was pacing to and fro with his machine gun. I was very nervous – I was sweating with nerves because I wondered what would happen if other Germans detected us. As soon as this guard turned round, I hit him on the head. I was very strong.

He immediately collapsed, screaming, but I shut his mouth and began to pull him along. After we'd dragged him for several metres the Germans opened fire, but we successfully got him back to headquarters about 8 kilometres away.'

The psychological impact of these snatch squads on the German soldiers was enormous. Helmut Walz, fighting in the rubble of Stalingrad, remembers once looking round to see that their medical orderly had disappeared from view: 'We called out, "Medical, where are you?" But he didn't answer.' During their search for him the Germans found a drain cover leading to the underground tunnels of the sewage system. Shocked, Helmut Walz shouted to his comrades: 'They pulled him down there!'

The pressure on the Soviet intelligence officers to get every scrap of useful information from these captured German soldiers was intense. An insight into just how such interrogations could be conducted during the war comes from Zinaida Pytkina. At first glance today she resembles one of the many grandmothers who trudge the streets of Russian provincial towns, wrapped like parcels against the biting wind. But her penetrating stare and directness of manner mark her out. For Zinaida Pytkina was selected during the war to serve in the most secret security service of all in Stalin's state – SMERSH. Until the fall of Communism she dared not tell even her own close friends just what she had done during the war.

So beloved of thriller writers, SMERSH (the Russian acronym stands for 'Death to Spies') actually did exist. Officially known as the Main Directorate for Counter-Intelligence, it was formed on 14 April 1943, three months after the Red Army retook Stalingrad, and replaced the so-called Special Departments of the People's Commissariat of Internal Affairs' Third Directorate. Their job, as Pytkina puts it discreetly, was 'to look after order' but 'silently'. As well as searching for enemy agents – and interrogating prisoners captured by the snatch squads – SMERSH also policed the loyalty of Soviet soldiers under the guise of investigating 'subversion'.

When Pytkina was told that she had been selected for SMERSH (she had not applied to join – they had chosen her) she was frightened. Perhaps, she thought, she had done something wrong: 'They look for offenders against the law, and I thought in the beginning that maybe I was a law offender too.'

When Pytkina was asked to 'describe her mission' within SMERSH she replied: 'My mission was to fulfil all the orders of my commanders.' But what did she actually do? 'Whatever we were told,' she answered. Only later did she become more forthcoming and admit that part of her job was to recruit informers inside the Red Army to spy on possible

deserters. Another of her tasks was to participate in the interrogations of German soldiers captured by the Soviet snatch squads – work she describes as 'hard, tricky and interesting'.

How, when interrogating captured German soldiers, could SMERSH officers tell if their captive was telling the truth? 'We knew in advance about the kind of information the officer had,' she replied. 'Both SMERSH and military intelligence already had part of the information that was expected from this German, and the rest was up to the specialist.'

'How did the "specialist" extract this information?'

'If he [the prisoner] doesn't answer, then we had to make him talk.'

'How did they make them talk? Did the Russians give the prisoners vodka?'

'I've never seen anyone being given vodka: just hit him or beat him,' she answered. 'Well, there's an enemy in front of me and this enemy is reluctant to give me what I want. If he gets a "wash" once or twice, then he will sing. This is why he was taken prisoner, to give information.' ('Wash', it transpires, was a euphemism for torture beatings. Later in the interview, when she was again asked, 'How did you make the Germans talk?' she answered even more equivocally and with deliberate irony: 'I don't know how to put it. Those who kept silent – they were treated "gently". No one wants to die.')

Zinaida Pytkina didn't just, on occasion, interrogate snatched prisoners but also took part in what could be the final stage of their journey through SMERSH – their execution. On one occasion she was told by her commanding officer to go and 'sort out' a young German major whose interrogation had been completed. Outside the interrogation building a pit had been dug and the German officer was ordered to kneel beside it. Pytkina drew her pistol ('My hand didn't tremble'), pointed it at his neck and pulled the trigger. His body fell into the pit. 'It was joy for me,' she says, describing her emotions at that moment. 'The Germans didn't ask us to spare them and I was angry…I was also pleased. I fulfilled my task. And I went back into the office and had a drink.'

When asked to explain in more detail why she felt this way after killing this German officer in cold blood, she replied: 'I am sorry for my people. When we were retreating we lost so many 17-, 18-year-olds. Do I have to be sorry for the German after that? This was my mood…. As a member of the Communist Party, I saw in front of me a man who could have killed my relatives…. I would have cut off his head if I had been asked to. One person less, I thought. Ask him how many people he killed – did he not think about this?…

OPPOSITE Zinaida Pytkina, a SMERSH intelligence officer who freely admits she killed an unarmed German prisoner.

'I understand the interest in how a woman can kill a man. I wouldn't do it now. I would do it only if there was a war and I saw again what I had seen during the war.... They had been captured, and people like him had killed many Russian soldiers. Should I have kissed him for that?... I even used to ask to be sent on reconnaissance missions to capture a prisoner, but it wasn't allowed. Women were not sent on such missions – but I wanted to go. I wanted to crawl to the enemy's side and to capture a prisoner, perhaps kill him.'

Stalin would have admired Zinaida Pytkina's ruthless logic, and back in the autumn of 1942 he called for similar cold-blooded determination from the defenders of Stalingrad. But determination alone would not win the battle. During the Germans' Operation Blue, the Red Army had demonstrated how they had mastered the art of retreating. Now they had to prove they could mount an effective attack. For the first time in the war the Red Army had to show that it understood how to prevail in a modern, mechanized war, and that they possessed tactical understanding as well as courage.

The first real sign of that change occurred in early autumn 1942 in Moscow. Stalin was on the telephone, and Zhukov and Vasilevskii (who was made Deputy Commissar for Defence in 1942) were discussing the strategic alternatives facing the Red Army in the south. 'Zhukov and Vasilevskii were talking to each other,' says Makhmud Gareev, who was a close colleague of Zhukov's, 'and Zhukov said, "We have to look for a new solution," and Stalin immediately overheard them, stopped speaking on the phone and asked: "Well, what solution do you mean?" Zhukov and Vasilevskii explained. Stalin said, "You've got a week to study the situation, but don't involve any other Stavka members."'

That conversation led to the first major Soviet victory of the war – Operation Uranus. The plan was ambitious: to attack the Germans from the flanks and encircle the entire 6th Army. Both the conception and implementation of Operation Uranus demonstrated that the Red Army had changed its approach from the desperate days of Kharkov five months earlier. 'They learnt from the Germans,' says Makhmud Gareev. 'They not only learnt from the Germans, but they learnt from their own mistakes.' The Uranus plan was inspired not just by the huge, pincer-like encirclements the Germans had mounted in 1941, but harked back to the theory of mechanized 'deep operations' which innovative Red Army commanders had proposed in the early

OPPOSITE Marshal Aleksandr Vasilevskii, the Soviet soldier who, together with Zhukov, masterminded Operation Uranus, the Red Army encirclement of the German 6th Army – the first great Soviet victory of the war.

1930s and which had subsequently been denounced. In accepting Zhukov and Vasilevskii's thinking, Stalin demonstrated both his flexibility and his cynicism – who cared if Soviet officers had been persecuted for suggesting similar ideas in the past? Perhaps the plan would work now.

The main thrust of the proposed Soviet attack would be not on the powerful German units of the 6th Army but on the Hungarian, Romanian and Italian soldiers who were stationed on the flanks. The Germans had been forced to use these armies from their Axis allies to fill in the gaps in their line – a situation that had arisen because Hitler had split his attacking force in two back in the summer.

Many of Stalin's previous operations had been distinguished by the ease with which the Germans had learnt of Soviet intentions, but Operation Uranus was different. This offensive was to become famous as the first example of the Soviet talent for military deception – *maskirovka*. Ivan Golokolenko was an officer in the 5th Tank Army who took part in Operation Uranus, and to start with even he and his comrades were deliberately misled about the true nature of the operation ahead. 'On 20 October 1942 we received an order to prepare wood for the frosty winter to help Moscow with supplies,' he says. His unit took the wood to a nearby train station only to discover that it wasn't destined for Moscow at all, but was needed to camouflage their tanks which were being loaded on to railway trucks. 'In the course of two or three days all three echelons travelled away – but no one knew in what direction we were finally going. We didn't know our destination; even the commander of the brigade did not know, and the station masters along the route did not know either.

'About 24 October we unloaded during the night at Kamulka station, north of Stalingrad. After that we travelled 55 kilometres without headlights. We travelled in complete darkness, very slowly, one car after another.... I remember at one of the crossroads there was a group of generals standing nearby, and one of the truck drivers felt at a loss and by mistake turned his front headlights on. He heard some swearwords and then the strike of a stick against the headlights and the sound of cracking glass. Then you could hear voices saying, "Zhukov! Zhukov!", and I could recognize Zhukov with the group of generals.' It was Zhukov himself who had smashed the headlights on the truck. 'He was there personally watching the progress of our convoys,' says Golokolenko. 'He was strict about camouflage and attached great importance to it. He would stop at nothing to achieve results.... He was cruel and merciless with people who disobeyed orders. I think it was necessary during that war.'

The concealment and deception of Operation Uranus went beyond merely denying the enemy knowledge of troop movements. Golokolenko's unit was one of many ordered to build trenches and other defensive fortifications in the open, so as to give the German reconnaissance planes the impression that an offensive was not contemplated. Bridges that the Germans could actually see from the air were deliberately built many kilometres from the proposed area of offensive operation: 'There were fake bridges as well as fake areas of troop concentration far from the direction of the attack. These bridges were built in order to distract the attention of the enemy from the direction of the main thrust.' When it was necessary to construct genuine river bridges for the forthcoming advance they were camouflaged: 'Some of the bridges were built as underwater bridges. They were built at a depth of 50 or 70 centimetres down in the water. From the air it was more difficult for the reconnaissance planes to spot the presence of such bridges.'

While they waited for the order to attack, Golokolenko's unit practised the coordination of infantry and tanks in offensive operations – incredibly, a task they had not undertaken before. They also trained to overcome one of their greatest fears – 'tank phobia': 'We had to sit in trenches and tanks travelled over us, and we soldiers were supposed to stay in the trenches without fearing the oncoming tanks.' The problem was a serious one: 'As soon as tanks appeared, our infantry would run away. This was a real scare. I remember also this fear of encirclement. As soon as somebody said, "They're about to encircle us!" this caused immediate panic.'

The Red Army also prepared a form of Blitzkrieg offensive that mirrored the one used against them in 1941 by the Germans. 'Previously tank units were used mainly as a support for infantry,' says Golokolenko. 'But this new idea was very different. At some narrow stretch of the front the defence would be broken and then through this narrow gap two tank corps would be introduced. The objective of the tank corps was to bypass the enemy's fortified areas and points of resistance and go deeper and deeper to capture the really important points like bridges or city towers. Infantry was supposed to follow the progress of the tanks and clear up whatever was left – this was the new thing.'

The Red Army also benefited from one of the most extraordinary and surprising achievements of the Soviet people during the war – their ability to out-produce the Germans in military hardware. The industrial facilities available to the Germans ought to have produced much more war

OVERLEAF The Soviets' ability to manufacture so much quality military equipment was a crucial factor in their eventual victory. Particularly feared by the Germans was the T34 tank, being prepared here in a Stalingrad factory in 1942.

material than a Soviet manufacturing base which had been disrupted by the invasion and the consequent need to relocate further east. Yet working in factories, often under appalling conditions, the Soviet workforce – half of whom were women by 1942 – utterly out-performed the Germans. In 1942, for example, they manufactured 25,000 aircraft – 10,000 more than the Germans managed to produce. And much of this military hardware (the later versions of the T34 tank in particular) was as good as or better than anything the Germans possessed.

In readiness for Operation Uranus the Soviets managed to assemble, undetected, a force of more than a million men. A measure of their success at deceiving the Germans is given by the comment of Zeitzler, Hitler's newly appointed Chief of the Army General Staff, on 23 October, less than four weeks before the launch of Uranus, that the Red Army were 'in no position to mount a major offensive with any far-reaching objective'.

At six o'clock in the morning on 19 November, the day on which Operation Uranus was to be launched, Ivan Golokolenko's unit knelt down before the banner of the brigade whilst an address from Stalin was read to them: 'There was something fatherly, something parental

A Soviet tank attack against the Germans near Stalingrad in 1942–3. By now the Red Army had learnt the tactics necessary to mount an armoured offensive.

about it. It said, "Dear generals and soldiers, I address you my brothers. Today you start an offensive and your actions decide the fate of the country – whether it remains an independent country or perishes." And those words really reached my heart.... I was close to tears when the meeting was over. I felt a real upsurge, a spiritual upsurge.'

No one can know just how many Red Army soldiers reacted to Stalin's message as Ivan Golokolenko did. One of the great unanswered questions of the war is whether Soviet citizens resisted the Germans out of fear of punishment if they didn't, out of patriotism, out of love of Stalin or out of faith in Communism. The answer, almost certainly, is a mixture of all these reasons, with different motivations surfacing not just in different people but in the same person at different times. But those of us looking back today are almost certain to underestimate Stalin's importance to the majority of the population of the Soviet Union. Given what we now know about Stalin's terror, it is easy to overlook the extent to which he was a powerful – almost a vital – focal point during the war. Typical of the views of many Soviet veterans today is Anatoly Mereshko's comment: 'What people say now about Stalin killing millions of people – we didn't know anything about it. And when we went into battle we shouted, "For Motherland! For Stalin!" Now we

have no ideology. There are no slogans that would bring the people together, like "Everything for the Front! Everything for the Victory!" A lot of women and children worked at the factories with this motto. It wasn't just hot air – it was based on people's beliefs.'

The artillery barrage that marked the start of Operation Uranus began at 7.30 a.m. on 19 November 1942. Just like the detailed training and deception that had preceded the operation, it too was conducted in a new way, and again in a Germanic style: 'Previously artillery was used for 10 or 15 minutes' shelling before the attack,' says Golokolenko. 'But now the big mass of the artillery – up to 500 artillery pieces – was relatively concentrated at a narrow stretch of the front, and all this mass was aiming at that narrow stretch of land with all its firepower.'

Golokolenko rode in a truck with his men to the front line: 'When I heard the artillery fire, it began to snow and the visibility got worse. Later that morning we heard the order to move forward. As soon as we reached the enemy's front line of defence, we came under very powerful fire. One of our tanks exploded, then another, and yet another caught fire. The truck in which I was riding was hit in the radiator. My men dismounted and ran after the tanks. They advanced about 300 metres and the tanks stopped and the infantrymen lay down on the ground.... I really felt horrible because in all my previous battles, like those near Leningrad, often when we started the offensive things began to go bad very quickly, and I was frightened that we would never learn to fight well, and so again when things went bad, when we began to fail, I also felt quite desperate and depressed.'

But his unit was just unlucky – it faced a part of the enemy line that had been undamaged by the artillery fire. Elsewhere other units had made good progress, and soon Golokolenko's brigade too was pushing on through the snow, advancing most often at night, further into German-held territory. The Romanians had been given the task of holding the flanks by the Germans, and their poor performance has been the subject of debate ever since. 'I don't want to hurt the feelings of the Romanians,' says Golokolenko, 'but they were less battle-ready than the Germans. The German Army was well trained and they

OPPOSITE A posed Soviet picture of a Red Army soldier at Stalingrad. What the propaganda didn't reveal was that the life expectancy of such a soldier could often be measured in hours.

OVERLEAF The civilian casualties at Stalingrad were immense. Not until the late 1980s were Soviet historians allowed to calculate the real death toll. Latest estimates put the figure at over 2 million. Few of the dead have a proper grave: the modern city of Volgograd (as Stalingrad was renamed) was literally built on their bones.

were braver. Romanians didn't have a real goal – what were they fighting for? You can't say that we went on without facing the enemy's resistance, but it was easier than it used to be. They didn't seem to have prepared any defensive areas.'

The main thrust of Operation Uranus was west of the River Don, more than 150 kilometres away from Paulus and Stalingrad to the north. Even if the Germans had responded quickly to the threat, it would have been hard for them to move their armour out to deal with the Soviet attack. But the Germans didn't act swiftly. Paulus's ability to react to the constantly increasing threat of encirclement was compromised by the necessity of consulting Hitler, who was taking time off from his headquarters in East Prussia and was staying at the Berghof in southern Bavaria. Those inadequate units that were sent by the Germans to counter the Soviet advance also had to deal with the snow

and the consequent poor visibility. The previous German advantages of surprise and lightning attack were lost.

In one of the legendary Soviet feats of the war, Lieutenant-Colonel Filippov and his men drove brazenly straight into the German-held town of Kalach with their lights turned off, and then, when they reached the bridge across the Don near the centre of the town, suddenly opened fire. This one dramatic action came to epitomize for the Red Army how far they had come, not just physically but tactically as well. They had beaten the Germans and their Axis allies

Some of the more than 90,000 German prisoners captured at Stalingrad. The vast majority died in Soviet captivity – a lucky few were returned to Germany in the 1950s.

not because of superior numbers, but because of superior thinking. On 23 November units of the Red Army met up near Kalach and completed the encirclement of the German 6th Army. 'We felt inspiration,' says Ivan Golokolenko. 'We felt confidence that we were capable of beating the enemy successfully, and this operation remained the most memorable – the brightest – event. I remember I felt as if I had wings, I felt as if I was flying. Before that I used to feel depressed, but now it was as if I opened my wings and I was capable of flying in the sky.'

Even though they knew they were encircled, many soldiers of the 6th Army refused to accept that they were in danger. The Red Army, they believed, was composed of inferior people, badly armed and worse trained. Moreover the Führer would not, could not, let them down. The last vestiges of the overweening confidence that had created the Barbarossa plan in the first place had still not disappeared. 'Stalingrad was surrounded,' says Bernhard Bechler, a German officer caught within the encirclement. 'But even then I believed that the Führer would not give us up; that he wouldn't sacrifice the 6th Army, that he would get the 6th Army out of there.' This faith in Hitler during the early stages of the encirclement was voiced by many surviving Stalingrad veterans. 'Everybody thought, well, this can't really last long,' says Gerhard Münch. 'It'll only last a few days – we thought this was a temporary situation.'

Hitler, no doubt influenced by his belief that his own 'will' had prevented a collapse in front of Moscow a year earlier, ordered Paulus to stay where he was and make no attempt to break out of the pocket. Göring, anxious as ever to curry favour with the Führer, boastfully promised that his Luftwaffe would supply the 6th Army by an 'air bridge'. There was a precedent; earlier in 1942, at Demyansk, German planes had successfully air-dropped supplies to troops surrounded by the Red Army – although the Demyansk operation was on nothing like the scale of the one proposed to keep the 6th Army functioning as an effective fighting force. Simultaneously, Field Marshal von Manstein was ordered to attack from the south-west of the front to cut a relief corridor through the Soviet encirclement and relieve Paulus. His Operation Winter Tempest began on 12 December 1942 and pushed on through the snow and sleet into the Soviet ring around Stalingrad.

When the men of the 6th Army learnt of the rescue attempt, they thought it concrete proof of the Führer's commitment to them. 'Allegedly Manstein was approaching,' says Bernhard Bechler. 'They kept telling us this story and sometimes people even imagined: "We've heard the roar of the guns of Manstein's army today – he must be near!" Suddenly these ideas were cropping up, although it wasn't true, but it was fear of the future that made people imagine these things.'

The Soviets had placed 60 divisions inside their ring around Stalingrad and Manstein's task was hopeless. On 19 December, the 57th Panzer Division reached the River Mishov 50 kilometres from Stalingrad – it was as near as the German relief force was ever to get. On Christmas Eve Manstein's own force was threatened with encirclement by the Soviet troops and withdrew.

As 1942 drew to a close it was also clear that the ambitious air bridge promised by Göring could provide but a fraction of the supplies needed within Stalingrad. Those German planes that did manage to get through often dropped their load on the Soviet positions because of wind conditions or a change in the position of the front line. Day by day, as conditions worsened for the 6th Army, their faith in the Führer's power to rescue them began to disintegrate.

'If you haven't experienced it yourself,' says Bernhard Bechler, 'you won't know how cruel it was. When I lay down and stuck my hand under the collar, my hand would be full of lice. And the lice carried typhus.... We had nothing to eat. There were some frozen horses and we took an axe and chopped some meat and heated it up in a pot just to have something to eat. We were just lying there, without any food, almost frozen to death, it was dreadful.... Just imagine the scene: steppe, everything frozen, sub-zero temperatures of minus 20 or 30 degrees, masses of snow. We were lying in dugouts in the snow... German soldiers were lying on the ground and German tanks ran over these soldiers because they were no longer able to get up and make themselves known. I was thinking to myself, subconsciously: if people at home could see us here, if they could only see our soldiers dying so wretchedly! And as I was thinking, I was beginning to have my first doubts, asking myself; what are you doing here at Stalingrad? What are you doing here, a German officer, thousands of miles away from home? Are you defending Germany in this place? And why?'

After Manstein's relief effort failed, and in the emotional atmosphere of Christmas and New Year in Stalingrad, some officers in the 6th Army were so desperate that they considered suicide. 'After our Christmas "party",' says Gerhard Münch, 'I went to the regimental staff to wish them Merry Christmas. Then I learned that officers of our artillery regiment had shot themselves.... And at New Year's Eve my own company commanders came to me and said that, since all of this did not make sense any more, and that everything was finishing anyway, shouldn't we all shoot ourselves together? We discussed for a whole night with each other what we should do. And at the end of this discussion it was clear that, as long as soldiers had to be led under our command, we did not have any moral right to commit suicide.'

That January Joachim Stempel visited his father, the general commanding the 371st Infantry Division (and a professional soldier before the war), who was fighting in a different section of the Stalingrad encirclement. The encounter would turn out to be one of the defining moments of Joachim Stempel's life: 'I drove to his command centre in a jeep and talked to him about the situation, about which as a divisional commander he knew more than I did as a small platoon leader. And so I realized how bad the situation really was. And my father said, very realistically, "We are being sacrificed in order to save others." And then the door opened and Paulus entered the bunker. My father reported to him and immediately said, "Should my son be sent out?" Paulus said no, that he might as well stay and listen to this. And then they discussed the situation. And Paulus finished by saying this: "My proud 6th Army is meeting a fate it does not deserve. For us, Stempel [he meant my father], the last road we have to take calls for strength, which we also have to ask of our men. As a German general, you know what is required of you at the end. My men and I will defend our position in the bunker until the Russians storm us, and then the bunker will be blown sky-high with us inside. I wish you all the best for your last stand." And he shook hands with both of us and disappeared.'

After Paulus left, Joachim Stempel and his father sat discussing what they had just heard. Its meaning seemed clear: 'My father too said that none of the generals would be taken prisoner – it's impossible, as the commander had said. "You try," he said. "You're still young. You try to get out of this cauldron, somehow to get through…. But I will shoot myself. I don't want to be a burden to my staff officers in their attempt to break through. I'm 50 years old, I can't be a burden to them. So I'll take care of it here. I will do it when the Russians are outside my bunker, here in this room in which you're standing…. I will act like a captain of a sinking ship. A captain doesn't get into the lifeboat, a captain goes down with his ship. And my men die here for their country, and will never see their homes again, and I won't see my home again either. I will stay here with my men."'

Joachim Stempel had one last conversation with his father: 'I thanked him for the way I had been raised and trained. For my schooling, the good home I'd had, the care I'd been given, and the opportunity to follow a career of my choice that I'd had. And I wished him all the best. And he said, as I saluted him with military honours, he said, "We'll see each other again soon, up there, where all brave soldiers meet again. Take care, my son." I saluted…and walked out to my friends.'

On 10 January 1943 the Red Army mounted Operation Ring to squeeze the noose tighter on the 6th Army, and by 26 January forward Soviet units had linked up with Chuikov's 62nd Army on the Volga. As January came to an end, so did the German resistance. 'One day three Red Army soldiers approached our little foxhole,' says Bernhard Bechler. 'We were living in there, my adjutant – a young lieutenant – and me. The regiment's command post was only a few metres away. Suddenly these Red Army soldiers were coming towards us. And we both thought in a flash, we don't have any ammunition, this is the end. They're either going to shoot us or they'll take us prisoner. What shall we do? At that point I saw my adjutant pull a photo from the pocket of his uniform jacket. I looked at it, and it was a photo of his young wife with two very young children. He glanced at the photo, tore it to pieces, pulled his handgun, shot himself in the head and was dead. I experienced it there and then, but one can't imagine what it's like when a person is suddenly lying there dying. The following moment the Red Army soldier was upon me. He held his pistol to my chest, but he didn't pull the trigger, and at that point, when I realized he wasn't going to shoot me, my second life began.'

As the German defence crumbled, Gerhard Münch, who only a few weeks before had counselled his junior officers not to commit suicide but to stay with their men as long as they were needed, received unexpected orders from a colonel at 51st Corps Headquarters. 'You are flying out, today,' he was told. Münch had been selected as one of the last 'special envoys' to carry documents out of Stalingrad. At the makeshift airfield desperate German soldiers milled around as Münch clambered aboard the plane. 'Then Russian artillery started to shoot at us and, as the pilot took off, soldiers who had not been able to get into the plane clung to the bottom of it. He tried to shake them off and they actually fell down. You can hardly describe it: you had to have seen it – all the hopes that these people had to get out of there.'

Münch had left his men behind in the encirclement – he had not even been allowed to telephone his own regiment to say that he was leaving them: 'It took me a long time, internally, to cope with it, the fact that I had not personally kept to the principle by which I had been brought up and educated – to stand by your men. It was very, very tough to cope with. It took me years…the soldiers believed in me and there was a relationship of trust, which is key for any soldiers' relationship. And then, in the last consequence, I am flown out.'

As the fate of the 6th Army became inevitable even to Hitler, he promoted Paulus to the rank of field marshal. No German field marshal had ever been taken prisoner. The message was clear – Paulus was expected to kill himself.

On 30 January, as Soviet troops closed in on Paulus's headquarters at the Univermag store on Heroes of the Revolution Square, Gerhard Hindenlang, one of his battalion commanders, received a radio message containing news of this promotion. Hindenlang was told to take the news to Paulus – along with the intelligence assessment that the Red Army was about to overwhelm the last German resistance: 'I went over and reported to the general and told him that on the radio we had heard about his promotion to field marshal. But I also had to say that at the same time I would have to ask him to capitulate because the Russians had positioned themselves around this store [his command post] and further defence was pointless. And he said to me, approximately, "Hindenlang, I am the youngest field marshal of the German Army and I have to become a prisoner of war." And I was a bit surprised – stunned even – to hear that, and he saw the surprise on my face and he said, "What do you think of suicide?" And I said, "Field Marshal, I lead troops and I will do so right until the last moment. I will go and become a prisoner of war if needs be, but you – you haven't got any forces any more." And he said, "Hindenlang, I'm a Christian. I refuse to commit suicide."'

The next day Paulus was captured alive by the Red Army. The minutes of Hitler's midday situation conference of 1 February 1943 survive, and demonstrate the combination of rage and bewilderment with which the Führer greeted the news: 'What hurts me so much,' he said, 'is that the heroism of so many soldiers is cancelled out by one single characterless weakling…. What is "life"? …the individual must die anyway. It is the nation which lives on after the individual. But how can anyone be afraid of this moment which sets him free from this vale of misery, unless the call of duty keeps him in this vale of tears!' Still later in the conference Hitler repeats his main theme. 'What hurts me the most personally is that I went on and promoted him to field marshal…. That's the last field marshal I promote in this war. One must not count one's chickens before they are hatched…. I just don't understand it…. He could have got out of this vale of tears and into eternity and been immortalized by the nation, and he'd rather go to Moscow. How can he even think of that as an alternative? It's crazy.' The transcript reveals a man almost in shock – less at the failure to hold Stalingrad than at the actions of Paulus.

For Günther von Below, who was Paulus's chief of operations and who went into captivity along with him, the field marshal's decision not to commit suicide is easy to

**ABOVE Field Marshal
Paulus in captivity at the
Spaso-Yevsinyev
monastery at Suzdali in the
summer of 1943. Because
of its relative comfort the
camp was nicknamed 'the
castle'. This photograph is
from the NKVD secret
archive.**

**OPPOSITE German helmets
piled high after the Soviet
victory at Stalingrad.**

explain. 'He [Paulus] said, "As a human being, and above all
as a Christian, I do not have the right to take my own life."
And my attitude was the same…. It wasn't cowardice. It was
quite simply our duty to go into captivity with our soldiers.
And if I had taken my own life there, that would have been
cowardice. That is my conviction.'

But the idea that Paulus, by not taking his own life, was able
to 'go into captivity' with his men is dismissed by Joachim
Stempel: 'It's just a joke, because minutes later the general was
no longer with his troops – he was in a heated fast train, with
white linen on the bed and table, on his way to the generals'
camp in Moscow.' Paulus was indeed separated from his men
– and photographs in an album still kept in the secret archive of the Russian Security
Service show the relative comfort of the field marshal's captivity. The conditions of his
imprisonment were, if not luxurious, certainly far superior to the degradation that
awaited his men in the Soviet camps. (Just over 90,000 German soldiers were taken

prisoner at Stalingrad; of these, 95 per cent of the non-commissioned officers and ordinary soldiers died, along with 55 per cent of the junior officers but only 5 per cent of senior officers.)

'I was disappointed,' says Joachim Stempel of his reaction to the news that Paulus had decided to allow himself to be captured. 'And I mistrusted everything. Because I thought, well, what is the word of a superior officer worth?' As far as Stempel was concerned, the conversation he had witnessed between Paulus and his father had been unequivocal – Paulus was calling on his senior officers to commit suicide. 'If my father had been uncertain in any way, he might have thought, well, OK, if Paulus, as commander-in-chief, survives and is taken prisoner, why should I, a divisional commander, not be taken captive as well?'

As Paulus was captured by the Red Army, elsewhere in Stalingrad Valentina Krutova and her brother and sister lay huddled in bed – by now too weak to scavenge for food: 'My brother was lying on one side of the bed, I was lying on the other side and my young sister was between us. The only thought we had was where to find something to eat. We were so hungry. I can't imagine now myself what I lived through…. We simply stayed in

bed and were lying all day silently; clinging to each other, hugging each other. Trying to keep our sister warm. We would turn our faces to her and press ourselves to her body.' Then, one day, they heard knocking at their door: 'And we could hear somebody shouting [in Russian], "Why are you knocking on the door? Don't knock. Maybe there are Germans inside, they'll shoot us. Throw the grenade." But one soldier did open the door, and to start with they couldn't make out who was inside. But we began to scream, "Don't kill us! We're Russians!" The soldier who was first to come in shouted, "There are children here." When they came in and saw us, they burst out crying.'

For the Red Army, the victory in Stalingrad was more than just a military triumph: it marked a spiritual watershed. 'I drank a toast,' says Suren Mirzoyan, 'and said after Stalingrad I am no longer afraid.' For Anatoly Mereshko, the victory gave him 'a supernatural, extraordinary feeling – that I won't be killed in the war. When I saw the surrendering Germans, and when I realized they hadn't killed me in Stalingrad, I felt I would live to see the victory. I felt confident. It was a real certainty that I would not die.'

But Stalingrad was not the single decisive moment of the war on the Eastern Front that is sometimes claimed. The Germans did not give up after this defeat, and the continued resistance of the 6th Army enabled the Germans to extricate Army Group A safely from the Kalmyk steppes and the Caucasus to the south, and thus avoid another encirclement. But the defeat at Stalingrad was none the less hugely significant. Never again would the German Army cast their eyes on the Volga. From now on they would begin their retreat west, step by bloody step.

OPPOSITE A rare, unposed picture of Hitler, taken in late 1942 or early 1943 – and he has a great deal to look pensive about. He had gambled that a swift Blitzkrieg would defeat the Red Army in 1941. Now Germany was involved in a world war against the USA, Britain and the Soviet Union.

VENGEANCE

At Stalingrad the Red Army had shown its courage and resilience. During Operation Uranus they had proved that in winter conditions they could tactically defeat the Germans. Then, at the Battle of Kursk in July 1943, they demonstrated for the first time that they could comprehensively drive back a German summer offensive. All this military success meant that Stalin had to decide how he should act towards those parts of the Soviet Union which had now been recaptured. Should he act with magnanimity, or should he act with vengeance? For a man of his character it was an easy decision.

That there had been some collaboration in the Soviet territories which had been occupied by the Germans is beyond doubt – there was no area in the whole of Europe that the Germans controlled, East or West, where the Germans had not received some help from the local population. When the Germans first occupied countries of the Soviet Union – from Latvia and Lithuania in the north to Chechnya and the Crimea in the south – they found many willing to help them, motivated often by the hope that the Nazis would support their nationalistic ambitions. The search for those guilty parties, their trial and subsequent punishment would have been understandable. Instead, in 1943 Stalin authorized the punishment by deportation of whole ethnic groups – effectively the movement of whole countries. They would all suffer – innocent as well as guilty. 'If Stalin had begun to sift things,' says Vladimir Semichastny, a post-war head of the KGB, 'and to discover who was guilty and who wasn't guilty, who fought at the front, who worked in the Communist Party organizations and so on, it would have taken 20 years. But the

OPPOSITE A victorious Soviet soldier in Berlin clutches a bust of Hitler. This picture was taken on 2 May 1945, just three days after the Führer's suicide.

OVERLEAF The Battle of Kursk, in July–August 1943, was a hugely significant moment in the war. The Red Army first held off Army Group Centre's summer offensive and then began to push them back. The action demonstrated to the world that the military initiative in this war now lay with the Soviet Union.

war was on, and if Stalin had begun to investigate, he might not have finished until now. This was Stalin's way to tackle problems. Start, and later we'll see who is guilty and who isn't…. It was purely Stalin's approach. To send away a million people meant nothing to him.'

The consequence of Stalin's 'approach' was suffering on a scale that is little known in the West. At the same time as Hitler was exterminating the Jews, so Stalin was turning his vengeance on many ethnic minorities within the Soviet Union. Thousands and thousands of innocent women and children died in one of the most brutal acts of ethnic cleansing in history.

One of the ethnic groups who suffered most were the Kalmyks. The Kalmyk steppe lies south of Stalingrad and stretches to the Caspian Sea in the east. This harsh world, poor in water, was settled by nomadic Mongols hundreds of years ago. The Germans had occupied the Kalmyk steppe when Army Group A had travelled through on their way south, advancing towards the Caucasus and the oilfields of Baku. For the German Army

their occupation of this unfamiliar Asian land had demonstrated just how far they had come, spiritually as well as geographically.

Now, with the Germans expelled, Stalin and his willing accomplice Lavrenti Beria, head of the secret police, the NKVD, decided that *all* the ethnic Kalmyks should suffer for the sins of the few who had collaborated with the enemy. (Significantly, they also decided that the ethnic Russian minority who lived on the Kalmyk steppe should remain there – an action that demonstrates the underlying injustice of the deportations.) In October 1943 Stalin confirmed the decision of the State Committee for Defence that the ethnic Kalmyks be

'relocated' to even remoter regions of the Soviet Union, such as Omsk and Novosibirsk in Siberia. In December, troops of Beria's NKVD moved down to the Kalmyk steppe to carry out the forced deportation. Amongst them was Lieutenant Nikonor Perevalov: 'We were told why the Kalmyks had to be evicted – because they had shown such a negative side of their character during the German occupation…. I saw them as someone on the enemy's side, not just because I was a Communist but from a personal point of view as well. But at the same time, when we looked at them, I thought: how could these people be capable of acting on the enemy's side? Because they looked quite miserable and pitiful.'

Beria's troops spent some days reconnoitring the area, checking how many lived in each house and whether they had guard dogs. Then, on 28 December 1943, a day that will be infamous for all time to the Kalmyk people, the NKVD acted. 'All of a sudden at six o'clock in the morning armed soldiers came in and said we were to be evicted,' says Vera Tachieva, who was a student at a teachers' training college. 'I felt numb – I didn't know what to do. All of a sudden my best friend burst out crying. At the college there were a lot of people shouting, screaming, crying. They assembled us in one building. All the girls were crying and weeping, we were in such a state. Some were losing consciousness. We were children – 17 or 18 years old only.'

'At four in the morning there was a loud knock at the door of our flat,' says Evdokiya Kuvakova, who was a young child at the time. 'Soldiers came in with machine guns. They told us to wake up and get ready…. My mother was so stunned that she couldn't do anything. After some time a soldier with a machine gun came up to us – he probably felt sorry for us – and said: "Don't worry, we're not going to kill you – we're going to relocate you." They said the Kalmyks had to be moved – and so as a child I became a traitor to the Motherland.'

'There must have been three children under 16 and a husband and wife,' says Nikonor Perevalov of the family he burst in upon that morning. 'They were all frightened. I said to them, "You are going to be evicted. You are to be put on lorries and taken to the assembly point." They were just standing, numb…. When you look at such backward, such brow-beaten people, and you see that this Kalmyk is incapable of doing anything bad, cannot attack you, together with the meagreness of their life, it makes you feel pity for them…. We were under oath to fulfil that order, but at the same time we thought how can it be that a whole people should be deported? The majority of the people were women, children and old men – why should these people suffer and be punished by Soviet law? Why did they have to suffer because of those who were really guilty?'

The Kalmyks were transported to train stations to begin their journey to the remotest parts of the Soviet Empire. Whole families had been given just two hours to pack their lifetime's belongings. Many who had been away from home that night were separated from their families and could not be certain they would ever see them again. On the trains the conditions were reminiscent of the infamous Jewish transports of the Nazis: 'They locked us up. There was shouting, crying, a lot of noise,' says Vera Tachieva. 'Some probably thought we would be killed. Some were crying, "They will destroy us." Some were crying, "It hurts." Some people were fighting for a place to sit or to lie because somebody's granny was ill. Mothers were crying because they didn't have anything to give their babies…. We couldn't understand. What was my fault? What was the fault of those five-year-olds? Unselectively, both the guilty and the innocent ones were deported, and I wondered whether they wanted to destroy the whole nation.'

Nikonor Perevalov might have had doubts when he saw that he was involved in an act of ethnic cleansing that included even women and small children, but it never occurred to him to disobey his orders: 'I thought I was doing the right thing because my senior officer ordered me to do it,' he says. 'It was my duty to fulfil his orders.' His response was particularly revealing because he thought it sufficient to retreat behind the simple defence – discredited at the Nuremberg war trials – that he was merely 'acting under orders'. Like Zinaida Pytkina, the lady from SMERSH (see page 165), Perevalov needed no further justification for his actions than an order from his superior – he even explained how he believed he must, without question, obey any criminal orders given by his commanders: 'I wasn't supposed to think about whether these were criminal orders or not criminal orders. The commander was the one and only commander; subordinates were supposed to fulfil his orders.' Such straightforward logic led to this chilling exchange filmed during the interview.

'What are the limits to your orders?' he was asked. 'If you had been ordered to shoot them [the Kalmyks] down, what would you have done?'

'If we had been ordered to shoot them down, we would have shot them down. I would have fulfilled this order. I remind you again, this is the requirement of the oath that we all swear and this is the rule.'

'If you had been ordered to, you would have shot down innocent women and children?'

'Yes.'

So, even though Nikonor Perevalov says that at the time he felt pity for the Kalmyks, he still admits he would have acted as Hitler's Einsatzgruppen did and murdered innocent women and children in cold blood. What his honest answers demonstrate is that in Stalin's Soviet Union any order, no matter how bizarre, criminal or illogical, could be carried out by Beria's men. And this goes some way to explain the treatment they meted out to Kalmyks like Aleksey Badmaev.

As an 18-year-old, Badmaev had fought with the Red Army on the Stalingrad front in the autumn of 1942, and had received awards for his bravery in defence of the Motherland. After being wounded, he was recovering in a military hospital in Stalingrad in January 1944 when he was ordered to report to the train station. He was deported north, to a labour camp in the Urals, along with thousands of other ethnic Kalmyks serving in the Red Army. 'Of course we were shocked,' he says, 'but what could we do? Everyone in the camp was saying that they believed we were traitors. No one believed we had been fighting and shedding our blood.' The apparent illogicality of deporting to a labour camp thousands of brave soldiers who had been fighting in the front line against the enemy is encapsulated by the fate of one of Badmaev's school friends who was imprisoned with him – a soldier who had been made a Hero of the Soviet Union. 'He was

Lavrenti Beria, head of the Soviet secret police and the man who masterminded the plan for the ethnic deportations – but only after his master, Stalin, had approved.

a strong man,' says Badmaev, 'but he broke down very quickly. He was emaciated and he lost half of his weight – he went from 80 kilograms to 49 kilograms. He died in the camp hospital. He was wearing his Order of the Red Banner and I remember him saying to me, "If I stay alive I'll kill everyone." I asked him who he wanted to kill. He replied: "Stalin and Beria."'

Conditions in the camp were so bad that another of Badmaev's comrades tried to survive by eating vermin. 'He had the bunk bed on top of me and I could hear him eating at night. I asked him, "What are you eating?" and he said, "Oh, no, you won't like this stuff." And he showed me a rat. A fried rat, grilled on the fire. I said, "No, I won't, I'd rather die." But he ate it. He died none the less because they soon ran out of rats…. He used to fight on the Caucasian front – he too had a medal for valour.'

The conditions inside the labour camp were bad enough to cope with, but the sheer senselessness of Stalin and Beria's action also weighed on Badmaev's mind: 'Of all people, I know very well that we were short of soldiers on the front, and to take these people [the Kalmyks] away was beyond stupidity. And secondly, the deportation of the whole nation was a crime. To punish one innocent person is enough of a crime, but to deport the whole of the people and to doom them to dying of extinction – well, I don't know what to compare it with.'

Life was scarcely better for the women and children sent to Siberia. On the five-day train journey north, Vera Tachieva watched as the weaker Kalmyks around her began to die. 'It was frightening because we had never seen dead people.... And we had to wait with the corpses in the train wagon until they were removed at the next station.' Tuberculosis, chronic dysentery and the cold all took a devastating toll. Once she looked through the slats of the wagon and saw a terrifying sight: 'I thought at first they were logs. But they were bodies piled up. Another girl said to me, "Can you see their hands and feet?" And indeed I could.' Such was the secrecy of the operation that the exact number of Kalmyks who died on these terrible train journeys may never be known. An idea of just how high the mortality rate could be is given by the figures available for just one of the regions of Siberia to which the Kalmyks were sent, Altai Krai, where out of 478 people on the transport 290 died on the journey.

Conditions for those Kalmyks who made it to Siberia were appalling. Vera Tachieva was sent to work in a munitions factory, living in a camp nearby: 'People suffered from hunger, died of under-nourishment. What did they feed us with? We got some thin porridge, and this porridge was a treat. People were not allowed to leave – they had nowhere to go to get food. This is why their bodies got swollen and they died – especially older people.'

Evdokiya Kuvakova was just five years old when she arrived in Siberia with the rest of her family, but the bitter memories remain strong: 'The worst was when we got there and got off the train into the snow. And I remember I was sitting in the snow and a local family had to pick us up but no one wanted to. It was January in Siberia, the coldest month. There was a strong wind which was very hard to bear. My mother was a dressmaker and this is what helped us survive. Those who had belongings swapped them for food. Those who didn't have anything to swap for food and didn't know Russian went begging, and a lot of people died from starvation.' Evdokiya Kuvakova's young brother died after only a few months in Siberia: 'My brother had to sleep on the floor. We were short of beds and the temperatures were very low, and he caught a bad cold which developed into pneumonia and he died. He was the only male descendant of the family, and my mother was so desperate that she felt suicidal.'

Not until after the death of Stalin were the Kalmyks 'rehabilitated' and allowed back to their homeland. Even then they could not speak openly about their suffering, and no monument to their dead was raised in Elista, the Kalmyk capital, until 1989. But in the dark days of their exile they composed a secret lament about their plight, the final words

of which are: 'Let Stalin's ashes be eaten by dogs.' 'I think these are very just words,' says Evdokiya Kuvakova.

The 'official' figure is that around 93,000 Kalmyks were deported, although many of those who suffered exile say that this number is a gross underestimation. The Kalmyks were only one of a number of national groups who were deported. Others included the Karachai people from the North Caucasus (68,000 deported) and the Chechens (500,000 deported). Beria himself wrote to Stalin asking for permission to deport additional groups, such as the Balkars from the Caucasus (340,000 deported) and the Tatars from the Crimea (180,000 deported). The precise total of those deported may never be known, but it is certainly much more than a million.

A letter from Beria to Stalin dated 24 February 1944 demonstrates how ultimate responsibility for all this human horror rests with the Soviet leader himself. It includes the line, 'If you give consent, I will be able to make all preparations necessary for the deportation of the Balkars on the spot before returning to Moscow.' In December that year Beria asked Stalin if awards could be given to some of those NKVD soldiers who had taken part in the deportations; Stalin agreed.

Beria's actions during the deportations are consistent with the overwhelming desire he manifested throughout his career to do whatever was necessary to please his boss. But there was more to Beria's usefulness to Stalin than mere sycophancy. Within the Stalinist system Beria was the person most able to exploit his master's suspicion, paranoia and desire for vengeance on his enemies – real and imagined.

An insight into how Beria performed such an extreme function within the Soviet state is given by Vladimir Semichastny, who during the war was a member of the Communist Youth League, the Komsomol, and who in the post-war era became head of the KGB (as the NKVD was renamed). In 1952 Semichastny was in charge of sports activities in the Komsomol, and was one of a group of Communist Party members held responsible for the performance of Soviet athletes at the Helsinki Olympics. The Soviet team had been narrowly beaten by the Americans in the overall medal table. On their return from Helsinki, Semichastny and the rest of the committee were driven straight to the Kremlin and ordered to explain themselves before a group of senior party members which included Georgy Malenkov, the Deputy Prime Minister, and Beria himself.

OPPOSITE A Cossack in German uniform. During their occupation, the Germans recruited thousands of people from Soviet ethnic minorities to their cause. As Stalin recaptured the occupied territories, he punished the innocent majority as well as the guilty minority.

'We were very frightened when we learnt Beria would be present,' says Semichastny. 'It was about ten or eleven o'clock at night when in the Kremlin we began to be questioned about the results of the Olympic competitions.... It was Beria who was the most tactless and the rudest – he was beside himself with rage. He was presenting himself as the supporter of Soviet sport, a person who cared that Soviet sportsmen win, and we were displayed as people who didn't care – but in fact it was pure falsification and provocation.' Beria turned on the delegation, saying, 'They should not have brought you here to the Kremlin but to a very different place,' by which they understood him to mean the NKVD prison cells. 'He even went so far as to reduce the leader of our delegation to a state where he couldn't answer elementary questions – like how many women were in the team. And Beria reacted to that in a very rowdy way.' The first part of the discussion ended with Malenkov announcing a break. He returned half an hour later and said, 'I've just talked to Comrade Stalin and he was quite pleased with the result of our performance at the Olympic Games.' As a result, Semichastny and the rest of his committee escaped Beria's wrath.

Semichastny's encounter with Beria is instructive. It demonstrates not only how unjust the system was ('People were sent to prison for telling jokes,' says Semichastny, 'so to lose a football game was a major crime by comparison') but also how Beria's rage made it easier for Stalin to punish the recalcitrant if he chose to. Just as Hitler always wished his generals to be like 'dogs straining on the leash' (and in this they often failed him in his eyes), so Beria must have been useful to Stalin; the leader of the NKVD always presented the option of repression. But Semichastny's brief experience in the Kremlin also demonstrates once again that Beria was there to provide a service to his leader – no more. It was Stalin who decided not to persecute Semichastny's delegation, just as it was Stalin who ultimately decided to persecute the ethnic minorities as the Red Army liberated the occupied territories of the Soviet Union. Stalin wanted to demonstrate that any ethnic or national group within the Soviet Union which tried to go its own way would be crushed – and punishing them all, guilty as well as innocent, was the most effective way of making the point.

At the same time as Stalin was wreaking his vengeance upon the ethnic minorities of the Soviet Union, so Hitler was concluding a far better-known campaign of hatred against a people he saw as the greatest threat to his own Empire – the Jews. By the time Stalin launched his operation against the Kalmyks at the end of 1943, the Nazi extermination policy of the Holocaust had been in full swing for nearly two years. The shooting of

Jewish men in the newly occupied territories had begun in the early days of Barbarossa, and swiftly escalated during 1941 to include the murder of Jewish women and children as well. The killing grew worse and worse, all in the context of the blood-lust of the Nazi war of annihilation against the Soviet Union. Experiments with gassing had begun in the autumn of 1941, and this led in the spring of 1942 to the establishment of special extermination centres such as Treblinka, east of Warsaw.

Because the killings of the Holocaust are horrific almost beyond comprehension, and since Hitler and the Nazis persecuted the Jews from the moment they came to power in 1933, it is tempting to lift the Holocaust out of its historical context of Hitler's war in the East. This is a mistake. Contrary to popular belief, the Nazis had no concrete plans to exterminate all the Jews before Operation Barbarossa was under way. Despite the fact that in his infamous speech of 30 January 1939 Hitler had said that if there was a world war it would mean 'the annihilation of the Jewish race in Europe', even one year into World War II the general policy was still to rob the Jews and then imprison them in ghettos prior to deporting them; there was even a proposal in existence in 1940 to send them to the island of Madagascar, to which the Germans now had access as a result of the defeat of France. Conditions for the Jews in a Nazi-controlled Madagascar would have been appalling and the intention ultimately genocidal, but the Holocaust as we know it would not have occurred. It was the catalyst of Operation Barbarossa that allowed what the Nazis called this 'radical' solution to the 'Jewish problem' to become possible.

We can never look inside Hitler's mind and know his exact motivation for authorizing the 'radical' extermination policy when he did (almost certainly some time between September and December 1941). Many factors would have played a part – his abiding conviction that the Jews were 'racially dangerous' to Germany, his belief that the Jews had 'betrayed' Germany during World War I, the invasion of Poland which brought 3 million Jews under Nazi control, and his belief that the newly occupied territories of the East should be 'cleansed' of Jews and Communists. But the idea of vengeance was also important. As Arnon Tamir, a German Jew who escaped to Palestine, put it, Nazi anti-Semitism can be summed up in the simple words, 'The Jew is guilty, for everything, always.' As early as 21 March 1933, less than two months after Hitler had become Chancellor, a Leipzig newspaper stated: 'If a bullet strikes our beloved leader, all the Jews in Germany will immediately be put up against a wall and the result will be a greater blood bath than the world has ever seen.'

By the spring of 1944, just as those Kalmyks who had survived the deportation began their lives of exile, Hitler was using a typical excuse to explain Germany's dire situation at this stage of the war – the Jews were to blame. Even though by now he had presided over the extermination of most of the Jews in the Reich and in the occupied territories, he still saw those who remained as responsible for the problems Germany faced. Hitler's dealings with his ally, Hungary, are the clearest example of this twisted thinking. After the German capitulation at Stalingrad and the disastrous defeat of Hungarian forces at Voronezh in January 1943, when the Hungarians lost 150,000 of their 200,000 soldiers to the Red Army, the new Prime Minister of Hungary, Laszlo Bardossy, tried to remove his country from its alliance with Nazi Germany. No new Hungarian troops were sent to the Russian Front in 1943, and peace feelers were put out to the West. Admiral Horthy, Hungary's leader, had refused during 1942 and 1943 to cooperate with the Nazi extermination policy and deport Hungarian Jews. So it was no accident that when, in March 1944, Hitler finally ordered German troops to occupy Hungary, he first blamed the Jews for the Hungarian lack of support to the Nazi cause: 'The Jews, who control everything in Hungary, and individual reactionary or partly Jewish and corrupt elements of the Hungarian aristocracy, have brought the Hungarian people, who were well disposed towards us, into this situation.'

Admiral Horthy was summoned to meet Hitler at Klessheim Castle on 18 March. As Hitler accused Horthy of duplicity, German troops entered Budapest. A new Hungarian regime under Dome Szotjay (although with Horthy remaining, alongside a Reich Plenipotentiary) began to comply with the Nazis' demands to implement the Final Solution. The Jewish deportations in Hungary in 1944 were swifter than in any other country in Nazi-occupied Europe. Under the personal supervision of Adolf Eichmann, Chief of the Jewish Office of the Gestapo, the deportations began in May 1944, and within ten days 116,000 Hungarian Jews had been transported to Auschwitz – more than had been sent from France in two and a half years. Hitler's vengeance was brutal and quick.

Israel Abelesz was 14 years old in 1944 and living with his mother, father and four brothers and sisters in the Hungarian provincial town of Kapovar. Their town was one of the last to be 'cleared' of Jews. At six o'clock in the morning on 18 June Hungarian police, acting on German orders, knocked at their door and gave

OPPOSITE Hitler in March 1944, when he ordered German troops to enter Hungary to secure the front and enforce the Final Solution on the country's Jewish population.

OVERLEAF Hungarian Jews in Budapest in the summer of 1944 when the deportations were in full swing.

them an hour to get their belongings together. 'It was terrible,' he says. 'The feeling that we were going away from this house, which was my grandfather's house, and we didn't know whether we would ever return.' Like the other Hungarian Jews who were deported, those of Kapovar were first robbed of their valuables and then transported via holding camps to Auschwitz.

As Abelesz discovered, in order to survive, however temporarily, in Auschwitz it was necessary to pass almost continuous selection: 'Within minutes of arrival they said men have to be in a separate row and women and children in another. I said to my 11-year-old brother, "You go with Mummy. I am already a grown-up – I am a man and I will go with my older brother and father." I saw he went with my mother, and within seconds they disappeared from sight.' His father was then ordered by the SS to go with his wife and their youngest son. Unbeknownst to them at the time, they had been selected for the gas

BELOW, LEFT Hungarian Jews arrive at Auschwitz-Birkenau in 1944. After days in a cattle truck, they are frightened and bewildered.
CENTRE The selection of new arrivals. Those thought fit to work are sent to one side of the arrivals platform; those of no 'use' (mostly women, children and old people) are sent to another.
RIGHT The selection is complete. Those on the left are destined, almost certainly, for immediate death in the gas chambers. Those on the right will become slave workers – and their life expectancy is measured in months.

chamber and immediate death. Israel and his brother, as potentially fit workers, were sent to a crowded barrack room: 'There were no beds – just a concrete floor. There was not enough room to stretch – you had to sleep sitting, one in each other's lap…. It was worse than being an animal – you had no identity, nothing; just like pigs who are fed in a trough. And it was a terrible feeling thinking what is going to happen.' In the barracks there was still constant selection. 'In the middle of the day they would come and select people to work. And after a few weeks we asked people who had been there longer about what was happening, and they said, "Look, nobody comes out of here alive at the end of the day."'

Israel Abelesz had been lucky in the initial selection, but as a small 14-year-old his luck did not seem likely to last for long. At the next stringent selection the worst happened: 'I was picked out because I was small. But as I was picked out I started running away. The Germans were doing selections with the Kapos – the criminals and Jewish collaborators who were leaders in the camp. And somebody said to one of them, "Go and get him," and he ran after me. I was running as fast as I could. When the Jewish collaborator caught me he said, "Run away from me!" – he didn't need to tell me twice. And then this larger Kapo, a horrible German criminal with a huge stick, ran after me. I was lucky that some Russian prisoners of war who were also in the camp came towards me. And after I ran

through them the Kapo stopped. He wasn't an SS man, so the Russians were not afraid of him – they could beat him up. So then I was just hiding among the people who were not selected.'

Once the selection was finished, normally no immediate danger remained. But this time 20 or 30 of those who had been selected managed to open the barrack door and run back into the main camp – with potentially deadly consequences for Abelesz: 'What did the Germans do? They picked up that amount from the rest of us so the number should fit. In fact I was picked again. When they counted us, I had tried not to draw attention to myself – that I was so small – by standing on some bricks in the middle of the group. But they picked me out again. But I started to beg in front of the German that I am strong, I can work. The Kapo gave me a slap in the face but the SS man said, "Ach, leave him," and they took somebody else instead of me.'

Incredibly, shortly afterwards he survived yet another selection: 'The third selection happened in the barracks. So I knew which barrack had already passed the selection, and I went there and stayed with those who had already passed.' Yet another stroke of luck was that after Abelesz had managed to escape selection until the end of 1944, the gassing stopped at Auschwitz because the Red Army was near. Together with the remaining inmates he was moved out of the camp on a forced march. Finally, he was able to dodge the guards once more and escape. 'Look,' he says, 'why I survived and others did not is a puzzle. I don't know why. I had a chain of luck…. I am a freak. I really should not have survived. My place is not in this world. It has occurred to me that someone will stop me and say, "Hey, you shouldn't be here! You shouldn't be among the people who lived – you should go back there again!"'

To the Nazis it was certainly a mistake that Israel Abelesz or any of the other Jewish inmates of Auschwitz survived. The selections were designed to be only a postponement of death. As it is, of the 440,000 Hungarian Jews sent to Auschwitz, 290,000 were murdered – including almost every one of the children. The swift killing of such a huge number almost overloaded the camp's extermination capacity. At the Auschwitz trial in Frankfurt after the war Hermann Langbein, a former inmate, stated in evidence: 'In 1944 children were thrown alive into the big fires that were burning near the crematoria. We heard about that in the main camp, and I told the garrison doctor, Dr Wirths, who refused to believe me. He went to Birkenau [the site of Auschwitz's gas chambers] to check…the next day, he simply said: "It was an order of Camp Commandant Höss." It was given because there was no longer enough gas.'

After the Swiss press publicized the deportations in June 1944, international pressure on Horthy grew. Defying Hitler once again, he ordered the deportations to stop – although not before more than two-thirds of Hungary's Jews had been sent to Auschwitz.

Both the Kalmyk and Hungarian deportations in 1944 show the depth of hatred and vengeance that existed in both Stalin and Hitler towards those groups who were held responsible, however unfairly, for hindering the war. Both dictators diverted valuable resources from the effort of fighting the enemy to deal with these people – including large numbers of women and children – whom they perceived as 'enemies within'. Both these case histories demonstrate how ideologically driven the war in the East could be, and show how easy it is for whole groups of people – be it the Mongol Kalmyks or the Jews of Hungary – to be demonized and treated barbarically under the broad cover of war. We need look no further than the ethnic cleansing in Kosovo in 1999, which intensified so dramatically once the NATO bombing had begun, to see how, when war occurs, natural enmities can be fanned and the 'solutions' to ethnic problems that have festered for years can suddenly become more radical.

But the deportations of the Kalmyks and the Hungarian Jews are not conceptually the same. The Kalmyks suffered greatly but there was some chance of survival, and once the survivors were 'rehabilitated' in the mid-1950s and allowed to return home, the nation could be re-formed, albeit with this grievous blight on their history. For the Jews of Hungary there was no such hope – two out of three of those deported were exterminated in the gas chambers of Auschwitz. (The Jews of Poland suffered an even greater rate of loss – more than 90 per cent of them were murdered. They had the misfortune to be amongst the first group of Jews whom the Nazis had turned upon.) Those Jews who did survive the Holocaust were, as Israel Abelesz says, simply 'lucky'. It was never the Nazis' intention that any of them should survive more than a matter of months. The American historian Charles Maier compares the Holocaust with Stalin's terror in these words: 'Nowhere else but in German-occupied Europe from 1941 to 1945 was there an apparatus so single-mindedly established to carry out mass murder as a process in its own right. And not just mass murder but ethnic extermination – killing, without even a pretext of individual wrongdoing, an entire people (if gypsies are counted, two peoples), including its children and its aged. The Russian system was wantonly brutal, cynical in its demand for punishment and confession, cruel, sycophantic, a perversion of any ideals that once motivated the revolutionaries. And yet despite all the blood, it did not set out to exterminate as an end in itself.'

This difference in kind between the two actions was brought home to me as I listened in the Ukrainian countryside in the 1990s to another of Stalin's victims – a member of the UPA, the Ukrainian Nationalist partisans. He told of a life of persecution, of years in the gulag and, once he was eventually allowed to return home, of repeated harassment by the local police. But here he was in front of me, standing in an independent Ukraine with his son and grandchildren around him; all of them proud of how Stalin's cruelty had finally been overcome. I thought of the countries of Eastern Europe I had seen – Poland, Lithuania, Belorussia and the Ukraine itself, where there could be no such happy scene for the Jews today because instead of imprisonment or exile there had been only murder. I remembered Himmler's words of 5 May 1944, when he explained to a gathering of German generals why, in pursuit of the Final Solution, the Nazis had killed children along with their parents: 'If you say, "The men – that we understand – but not the children," then may I draw your attention to my earlier remarks. In this showdown with Asia we must accustom ourselves to the ground rules and consign to oblivion the morals of past European wars which are dearer and much closer to us. We are, in my opinion, even as Germans with all our deep, heartfelt, good-natured feeling, not justified in allowing the hate-filled avengers to grow up so that our children and grandchildren have to settle with them because we, the fathers or grandfathers, were too weak and too cowardly and left the children for them.'

As Himmler was speaking these chilling words, the Red Army was continuing its advance west towards Germany, their proximity to the Reich playing a part in the Nazis' desire to wreak vengeance on the Jews of Hungary as swiftly as possible. By now Soviet forces had recaptured the Ukrainian capital, Kiev, and were within striking distance of the Belorussian capital, Minsk. And that summer of 1944 Hitler would suffer his greatest military setback of the war, a defeat that would feed his nihilism still further. This defeat was not the successful Allied invasion of France on D-Day, 6 June 1944, but the less-publicized Soviet attack on 22 June against Hitler's Army Group Centre in Belorussia. There is scarcely a greater measure of the extent to which the Eastern Front has been ignored in the consciousness of the general public in Britain and the USA than the comparison between Operation Overlord in France and Operation Bagration in the Soviet Union: the former is famous in Western popular culture,

OPPOSITE **Heinrich Himmler, Reichsführer SS, and his daughter. This devoted father (and, as many of those who worked for him testify, kind and considerate boss) was one of the greatest monsters in all history, overseeing the mass extermination of millions, including hundreds of thousands of women and children.**

whilst knowledge of the latter is mostly confined to historians. Yet the Germans possessed just over 30 divisions in the West (excluding Italy) to meet the Allied invasion of Europe, whilst they fielded more than five times as many – 165 divisions – on the Eastern Front. And Operation Bagration would eliminate, on the German side, more than three times as many divisions as the Allies landed on D-Day. (It was Stalin who named the offensive Operation Bagration – after a military hero in the fight against Napoleon in 1812; like Stalin, Bagration was of Georgian origin.)

'The Belorussian operation was a classic,' says Makhmud Gareev, who as a young Red Army officer took part in the offensive. 'Everything was well thought through.' Stalin demonstrated how far he had come from the incompetent leader who had so catastrophically presided over the disasters of 1941 by the way he listened to the deeply held views of Konstantin Rokossovsky, commander of the 1st Belorussian Front, about the tactics which should be adopted in the operation. Rokossovsky believed that the Red Army should attack Army Group Centre in two equally strong strikes, from the south and from the north. Stalin, aware of the accepted theory which dictated that forces should not be split, told Rokossovsky to leave the room and 'think it over'. When the military commander returned, he repeated his view that there should be two strikes. Eventually Stalin let him have his way – no doubt aware that Rokossovsky must be committed to his plan since he knew the fate he would suffer if he was wrong; as a junior officer, Rokossovsky had been imprisoned and tortured during the purges of the 1930s.

The preparations for Operation Bagration also illustrated the extent to which the Red Army had developed the art of deceiving their enemy about their true intentions. The sophisticated Soviet deception (*maskirovka*) plan was evident from the highest level, where knowledge of the aims of the operation was restricted to a handful of senior officers, to the lowest, where individual units of the Red Army hid under camouflage during the day and moved only at night, observing the strictest radio silence. In other areas of the front line far from the designated point of attack (most notably the area of the 3rd Ukrainian Front to the south) Soviet forces would be moved into the area during the day in full view of German reconnaissance aircraft, and then secretly moved out again at night – only to be transported openly in again the next day. The Red Army intended to deceive the Germans both about the point of the intended attack and the size of the Soviet force.

OPPOSITE By 1944 the whole German Army knew that the great Nazi dream of the conquest of the East lay in ruins. The question now was: what would become of Germany and the people who had started the war?

**Konstantin Rokossovsky, commander of the
1st Belorussian Front.**

None the less, not even the Red Army could completely conceal the build-up during May and June 1944 of the 1.4 million soldiers who were about to take part in Operation Bagration. Whilst the intelligence gathered by the German Army Command (OKH) did lead them, falsely, to believe that the Soviets were planning an attack in the south towards the Balkans, by the end of May some units within Army Group Centre believed correctly that the main offensive would be directed against them. Hitler was not convinced. He ordered Army Group Centre to stand firm and, if attacked, to concentrate their defence around key Feste Plätze or fortified towns. In a directive of 8 March that year Hitler had stated that these Feste Plätze would 'fulfil the function of fortresses in former historical times. They will ensure that the enemy does not occupy these areas of decisive operational importance. They will allow themselves to be surrounded, thereby holding down the largest possible numbers of enemy forces, and establishing conditions favourable for counter attacks.'

The discontent felt by Army Group Centre at such orders from the Führer is evident from these words, written by the commander of the German 9th Army, General Jordan, in June 1944: 'Ninth Army stands on the eve of another great battle, unpredictable in extent and duration…the Army believes that, even under the present conditions, it would be possible to stop the enemy offensive, but not under the present directives which require an absolutely rigid defence…. The Army considers the orders establishing "Feste Plätze" particularly dangerous. The Army therefore looks ahead to the coming battle with bitterness, knowing that it is bound by orders to tactical measures which it cannot in good conscience accept as correct and which in our earlier victorious campaigns were the causes of the enemy defeats….'

'In 1944 we were advancing like the Germans used to advance in 1941,' says Veniamin Fyodorov, a Red Army soldier who took part in the initial assault of Operation Bagration

OPERATION BAGRATION
AND THE ASSAULT ON BERLIN

Front lines 1944

—— June 13

– – July 18

- - - August 29

→ Soviet advance

•••• Soviet front line 19 April 1945

—— Armistice line May 1945

Baltic Sea

Leningrad

ESTONIA

LATVIA

Riga

Moscow

LITHUANIA

Vilnius

Vitebsk

Smolensk

Königsberg

EAST
PRUSSIA

Kaunus

Minsk

USSR

Berlin

1ST BELORUSSIAN FRONT
(Zhukov)

Bialystok

BELORUSSIA

*Pripet
Marshes*

Kursk

1ST UKRAINIAN FRONT
(Konev)

Warsaw

Pinsk

GERMANY

Vistul

*Bug
a*

1ST BELORUSSIAN FRONT
(Rokossovsky)

Kiev

POLAND

Lvov

Prague

Cracow

Dnieper

SLOVAKIA

UKRAINE

1ST UKRAINIAN FRONT
(Konev)

HUNGARY

ROMANIA

*Black
Sea*

CROATIA

SERBIA

BULGARIA

0   300 km

on 22 June 1944, three years to the day since the German invasion. 'The German behaviour in their fortified areas was stupid…. Our shelling broke them down. Huge amounts of shells flew towards them and you couldn't hear anything; only this – booming! The fortified area could be smashed completely. It was death…. The Germans held the ground to the last man – they were all doomed to death.'

Heinz Fiedler was one of the German soldiers of the 9th Army ordered to hold the Fester Platz of Bobruisk in the face of the Soviet advance. Previous battle experience had made him cynical about such 'nonsensical' orders from the High Command: 'I remember once that one position had definitely to be taken back again, and the second lieutenant had refused to attack once more because more than half of his men had already died. And then they did attack, and they were all just sacrificed. They attacked again and again until the very last one died, and that of course makes you wonder. But those were the men of the General Staff. They had their little flags and they put them on the map and then they say, "This absolutely has to be restored, no matter what the sacrifices are."'

Harsh as Heinz Fiedler's past experience of the war had been, it was as nothing compared to life inside the besieged Feste Plätze: 'Everywhere dead bodies were lying – dead bodies, wounded people, people screaming. You didn't have any feeling for warmth or coldness or light or darkness or thirst or hunger. You didn't need to go to the toilet. I can't explain it. It's such a tension you're under…. We were encircled, and in front of us were Russian tanks dug into the ground so that all you could see were their round turrets. They were shooting like mad. They must have had so much ammunition it was incredible. And from our back you heard [from the Germans], "We don't have any fuel, we don't have any ammunition left." And that's what you heard all the time…. You have to think of the psychological burden on the individuals. I did not get married on purpose because – well, a widow with children will have difficulties in finding a new man when they already have limited means. But those who were married and who had two or three little children at home on the one hand, and on the other hand to fulfil this order [to stand fast] as an integral part of the unit – this psychological burden you cannot measure.' Heinz Fiedler admits he felt 'abandoned' and 'betrayed' by the High Command of the Army: 'Those in the Führer Headquarters have easy talking – it's easy to be clever when you're there, that's what you're thinking…. On the other hand you had this obedience that nowadays we are reproached with as being the obedience of carcasses, but the way the German Wehrmacht was you will never ever find again. You will never find such an Army again in this world.'

The Soviet 65th Army threatened to engulf not just the German forces holding out in Bobruisk but also other German units to the east. General Jordan of the German 9th Army, of which Heinz Fiedler's unit was part, raged at his superiors' stupidity: 'HQ 9th Army is fully aware of the disastrous consequences of all these orders,' says the 9th Army war diary. 'It is a bitter pill to swallow, though, when one feels that behind these Army Group instructions, which so utterly ignore one's own pressing suggestions, and behind the answers given by the Field Marshal and his Chief of Staff, one can see no sign of a commander showing any purposeful will to do his utmost, but just the execution of orders whose basis has long since been overtaken by events.'

Hitler, unhappy about the way General Jordan had deployed the 20th Panzer division during the battle and no doubt classing him as a typical 'cowardly wretch', relieved him of his command and appointed General Nikolaus von Vormann to take control of what remained of the 9th Army. But a change of command could not change the bare facts – which were that the Führer's own policy of Feste Plätze had proved disastrous. In Bobruisk the defenders were hindered by German troops, who had retreated into the town seeking refuge, leaving their heavy weapons behind. Permission was finally granted to attempt a break-out – but one division was still ordered to stay behind and fight to the last. 'Then the last command arrived,' says Heinz Fiedler. 'Destroy vehicles, shoot horses, take as much hand ammunition and rations with you as you can carry. Every man for himself – go on and rescue yourself!'

Few of those who attempted to break through the encirclement managed to reach the safety of the new German line further to the west. Most were either killed by strafing from Soviet warplanes or by the Red Army on the ground in the kind of slaughter reminiscent of the massive German encirclements of 1941. 'We tried to break out but we were getting fired on and then there was panic,' says Heinz Fiedler. 'There was a private, a young boy, who sat by a birch tree with his intestines streaming from his stomach, crying "Shoot me!" and everybody just ran past him. I had to stop but I could not shoot him. And then a young second lieutenant from the sappers came and gave him the *coup de grâce* with a pistol to his temple. And that's when I had to cry bitterly. I thought if his mother knew how her boy ended…instead she gets a letter from the squadron saying, "Your son fell on the field of honour for Great Germany."'

Heinz Fiedler was one of the handful who made it through the Red Army lines,

OVERLEAF As the Red Army moves inexorably West, these soldiers shake their fists at a German corpse. Their experience of this war had not made them magnanimous in victory.

but the mighty 9th Army was all but eliminated. In total Army Group Centre completely lost 17 divisions, with another 50 suffering losses of 50 per cent. 'Hitler's order to keep the Germans in the fortified areas and carry on fighting doomed the Germans to death,' says Fyodor Bubenchikov, a Red Army officer who took part in Operation Bagration. 'Instead of allowing the Germans to retreat, he actually left his people for you to destroy them…. Gradually the Germans were losing morale and losing their belief in victory. The Germans no longer cried, "Heil Hitler!" On the contrary, when they were surrendering they were crying, "Hitler Kaputt!"… We felt we were flying on the wings of victory… victory always makes everyone feel like this, from ordinary soldier to commander, and all our units were filled with this sensation.'

As the Red Army moved forward 'on the wings of victory', they began to liberate Soviet prisoners captured by the Germans earlier in the war. One of those whom they found was Tatiana Nanieva, a woman who still finds it hard to make sense of what happened to her during the war. Her hatred of the invading Germans had been total: 'I thought this was an invasion of our peaceful country and this was an enemy who should be wiped out – I reacted with great anger. Immediately war was declared I rushed like lightning to be drafted.'

A trained nurse and a devoted Communist, she was working in a forward field hospital on the south-west front in October 1942 when she was caught in an encirclement by the swift advance of the Germans in Operation Blue: 'There was no panic. We carried on bandaging. Even if a bomb exploded on the treatment table, we were supposed to continue. And then when the [German] tanks appeared, you could see them moving fast. Then I think it was the political officer who said, "Split up and run!" We had no more wounded to tend to.' She ran to a nearby hut where she managed to bury her Party membership card in the earth just before the Germans captured her. 'After that my life started spinning in large circles,' she says.

'The first moment which really frightened me was when we were taken to a camp in southern Poland. What paralysed me with fear was when they began to choose pretty girls. There were a lot of us – but there were a dozen or so who were pretty. You know a face is still pretty under dirt or grime. And they'd be taken away to satisfy their [captors'] needs. Then they'd be returned, so dishevelled. And they could be taken away again and again….' There were even occasions when the Germans committed rape in full view of the other women prisoners. 'A few of us were sewing, working in a large room in the camp. A German came into our room. "*Komm! Komm!*" he said, to one of the girls he liked the look of. And immediately, straight away, right by us, he spread her out and did what he had to, like a hound taking a bitch. As a man he did everything to satisfy himself. Then he spat at her. And she rose and came back all dishevelled, angry and humiliated. And he went off without a care…. We weren't people in their eyes. They had a completely different way of thinking. They were beings of a higher race who were permitted to do everything.' Nanieva herself managed to escape being raped only because the Germans thought other girls more attractive.

It was in January 1945 that the Red Army liberated her camp. They were greeted with joy and pride: 'They came with such pomp, singing songs. They walked so proudly with heads up…. Our feelings were joyful, elated, we believed that victory was at hand and that a normal life would begin again. I was yearning for my Motherland, for my family, and I really wanted to live so badly.' Two Red Army officers approached her: 'One of them was angry, all het up. "So how did you live it up here, then?" he said. "You whores!" And I became so hurt and replied: "You didn't even ask us how we existed whilst we waited for you!" I was a whore all the same in his eyes. He grabbed his pistol. The second – maybe he was less drunk or something – he signalled me to beat it: "Just run for it!" he said.'

Nanieva, along with the other women who had been prisoners of the Germans, was investigated by SMERSH. 'I was accused. Then they showed me the charge – I am accused under article 58b. I asked what does that mean? "Betrayal of the Motherland" was the answer. And that's when I cried. I never betrayed her. I loved her very much. I was ready to die for her, but at this point I cried for the first time.' Nanieva was sentenced to six years in the gulag and lifetime exile in Siberia.

As Tatiana Nanieva discovered to enormous personal cost, Stalin had decreed that there were no Soviet prisoners of war in German hands – only traitors. And that cruel logic was applied to this woman, a committed member of the Communist Party, whose only crime had been to volunteer to become a nurse in the front line, and then, through no fault of her own, to be captured by the Germans. She was one of at least a million Soviet prisoners who were imprisoned twice – once by the Germans and once by Stalin.

She was transported in a cattle truck, together with other former POWs, to the northern Urals: 'The gulag – you probably know about the gulag and all its horrors. I saw the deaths of clever people – many such people died. There weren't just political exiles there, but also criminals too. The drunkenness and all that went with it. And you think, you imagine that for the rest of your life it'll be like that. I wanted to die.'

Nanieva was regularly interrogated in the Soviet camp. One question was repeated again and again: 'What orders did they [the Germans] give you?' 'Even if you could tear yourself to pieces, you couldn't prove a thing,' she says. 'They didn't believe you. No one, absolutely no one believed you…. When the interrogator questioned me, that word [whore] was practically always hanging on the tip of his tongue…. The system was depraved. In the whole world there are always POWs, and it's impossible for there not to be. That's how it has always happened in history. But in our country they were not accepted. Because of that, we suffered a lot.'

Stalin, true to character, was not just suspicious of Soviet soldiers who had been captured by the Germans, but also looked with a jaundiced eye on the generals who surrounded him. The circumstances of the war had demanded that he allow them greater latitude in decision-making, but he had never trusted his military commanders completely. Now, as 1944 came to an end, there were signs that with victory in sight he was reverting to his old vindictive ways. In November that year he appointed Marshal Zhukov to command the 1st Belorussian front. This move is capable of two very different interpretations. Whilst it might appear that Zhukov was being given the 'honour' of leading the main assault on Berlin, he was also removed from the role he had gradually been making his own, as the Red Army's single military genius. Instead of masterminding the whole operation at Stalin's shoulder, Zhukov was now just one of several front-line commanders. 'When we were close to winning the victory,' says Makhmud Gareev, 'he [Stalin] began to have ideas that he was brilliant at all the questions of strategy and tactics…. He was also envious and jealous of Zhukov – he was always envious and jealous of people who rose high. He wanted to get the credit for everything himself.'

Political considerations also weighed more heavily with Stalin now than at any time previously in the war. Even though by early February 1945 Soviet forces were only 40 kilometres from Berlin, he delayed launching the final strike on the German capital for nearly two months. This wholly uncharacteristic inaction – impetuosity in military assault had, up to now, been characteristic of Stalin's military leadership – was in part caused by the need to eliminate German resistance in the Soviet rear, but it was also the result of Stalin's desire to maximize Soviet influence in the post-war world. Stalin wanted both to capture Vienna and assemble enough Soviet reserves not just to take Berlin but to deal with any subsequent problems that might be caused by the Allies – 'friends' whom he increasingly distrusted. Stalin reasoned, rightly as it transpired, that the Allies would

be unable to break through to Berlin until after April at the earliest and, in any event, by the time of the Yalta conference in February 1945, an agreement had been reached which left Berlin deep inside the proposed Soviet zone of occupied Germany.

As a result, it was not until 16 April 1945 that he ordered the final assault on Berlin. Even then, Stalin was careful to organize the attack so that no single general could snatch all the credit. Zhukov and Marshal Konev, the commander of the 1st Ukrainian Front, were *jointly* charged with the task of conquering the capital of the Reich. 'Stalin encouraged an intrigue – scheming,' says Makhmud Gareev. 'When they were drawing the demarcation line between the two fronts in Berlin, Stalin crossed this demarcation line out and said, "Whoever comes to Berlin first, well, let him take Berlin." This created

ABOVE Marshal Konev, commander of the 1st Ukrainian Front.

OVERLEAF A Soviet propaganda photograph showing the Red Army approaching the Reichstag in Berlin. What the Communist history didn't recount was the problems caused in the days before this picture was taken by the unclear demarcation line between Zhukov's and Konev's forces during the Battle for Berlin.

friction…. You can only guess Stalin was doing it so that no one gets stuck up and thinks that he was the particular general who took Berlin…. At the same time he had already begun to think what would happen after the war if Zhukov's authority grew too big.'

While Stalin was acting in a way that demonstrated his true character, so was Hitler. As his forces crumbled around him under the battering of attacks from both East and West, Hitler decided that the German people had demonstrated that they were unfit for his leadership. His vengeance would not be confined to Jews and other 'sub-humans' but would extend to all of Germany. In a Führer Order of 19 March he ordered the destruction inside Germany of anything 'that the enemy could use for the continuation of the struggle'. This command, which has come to be known as the Nero Order (*Nero-Befehl*), called for the same scorched earth tactics to be used on German soil as had been practised in the retreat from Moscow – and for them to be used at a time when defeat was inevitable. Albert Speer, the Nazi Armaments Minister, managed to minimize the effect of the order by insisting that its implementation be coordinated through his ministry, but the wording of the Nero Order itself is unequivocal. Hitler summed up his feelings at a military situation conference on 18 April when he said, 'If the German people lose the war, then they will have proved themselves unworthy of me.'

As Hitler sat in the bunker of the Reichschancellery and raged at the failure of the Germans to rise to the genius of their Führer, both Zhukov and Konev felt the consequences of Stalin's imposition of a 'race to Berlin'. Stalin now issued a map with a demarcation line through the city which left Konev 100 metres west of the Reichstag, the parliament building, which was the trophy that both Marshals sought. The armies of Zhukov and Konev, already engaged in fierce fighting street by street with the Germans, became entangled with each other at the imprecise boundaries between their sectors. Chuikov's 8th Guards from Zhukov's 1st Belorussian Front ran into Luchinskii's infantry from Konev's 1st Ukrainian Front.

Anatoly Mereshko served with Chuikov in the battle for Berlin as part of Zhukov's 1st Belorussian Front, and witnessed first-hand the desperate rivalry that flourished after Stalin had set his generals at each other's throats: 'Once Chuikov sent me to a particular suburb [of Berlin] to find out whose tanks were there. I got into my car with machine gunners, rode up there and talked to the people in the tanks. One said, "I am from the Belorussian Front," another "I am from the Ukrainian front." "Who came here first?" I asked. "I don't know," they replied. I asked the civilians, "Whose tanks got here first?"

They just said, "Russian tanks." It was difficult enough for a military man to tell the difference between the tanks. So when I came back I reported that Zhukov's tanks got there first and Konev's tanks came later. So the celebration fireworks in Moscow were in his name…. At that time it was a custom to arrange fireworks in Moscow with the announcement saying that "in honour of such-and-such

Red Army soldiers celebrate in Berlin. A war that the Germans had believed would last just a few months and be won by their unyielding Blitzkrieg was over only now – nearly four years after it had begun.

army capturing this suburb of Berlin there had to be fireworks".' Only on 28 April did Stalin finally authorize a Stavka directive that confirmed Zhukov could take the Reichstag himself.

When Hitler shot himself in his bunker on 30 April, the Red Army celebrated – including units stationed in the east German town of Demmin. Hitler's suicide had not satisfied the Soviet soldiers' desire for revenge, and they wanted every German to pay for the sins of the Nazis. One of the innocent Germans who suffered their vengeance was

Waltraud Reski, then an 11-year-old Demmin schoolgirl. As Berlin fell, she and her family heard this terrible news: 'Demmin was to burn for three days.... And the women were fair game for three days too – free to be abused.' Waltraud's own mother was raped many times by Soviet soldiers. 'All the women were disguised, but you can always see whether a woman has a good figure, and somehow they found my mother again and again and treated her terribly. And she never really recovered.... It's impossible to imagine what it is like to be raped 10 or 20 times a day, so that one's hardly human any more.... Both my sister, who is four years younger than me, and I, tried to shield our mother and screamed.... This feeling of helplessness and cruelty – even today I am unable to find words for it.'

Such was the desperation of the citizens of Demmin that hundreds ran down to the rivers that surround the town. 'I kept seeing women holding children by the hand. And they were running down towards the water...and many had tied themselves together and I was wondering: why are they doing that? ...I could hear it – there is a sort of splashing sound when a person jumps into the water – and so I kept asking: "Why are they jumping into the water?" And my grandmother said: "They are so unhappy, they want to take their own lives." ...And the sight of those who had gone into the water the previous night, those terrible sights, those bodies, reddish-blue and swollen. I didn't often look because I didn't want it to be true.' Her own mother, distraught at having just been raped once more, grabbed Waltraud and her sister and ran towards the river. 'And my grandmother kept saying, "Please don't do this! What are you doing? What am I supposed to tell your husband when he comes back from the war and you've gone?" And somehow she then became calmer.'

Several thousand townspeople committed suicide in Demmin during the Red Army's rampage. The exact number of Germans raped or killed by them in acts of revenge in the final months of the war, and in its immediate aftermath, will never be known. It is a figure certainly – at least – in the hundreds of thousands. Although some Soviet soldiers were later court-martialled for a small proportion of these offences, there is evidence that those in authority were capable of turning a blind eye to their actions. When Stalin was told how some Red Army soldiers were treating German refugees, he is reported to have said: 'We lecture our soldiers too much; let them have some initiative.'

The vengeance exacted by the Red Army on the people of

OPPOSITE A victorious and smug Stalin at the Potsdam Conference in July 1945. Now the Germans had been defeated, it was time for Stalin to grab the spoils in the form of the Communist occupation of Eastern Europe.

Demmin, perpetrated in the last hours of the war, is an appallingly appropriate end for a war that had begun nearly four years before with the unleashing of such terrible hatred by the Nazis on the Soviet Union. Now this hatred was rebounding on Germany. 'This must never happen again,' says Waltraud Reski. 'Not just the fighting against each other, but also this idea of the enemy not being human.'

A victory parade through Red Square was held on 24 June 1945. 'There were suggestions that it was Stalin who was going to inspect the parade,' says Makhmud Gareev. 'Stalin's son, Vasily, used to say that such was Stalin's plan...that Stalin was even practising riding a horse, but he fell off and so said he wouldn't inspect the parade. But

who knows whether Stalin really planned to do it?' In the end Stalin decided that Zhukov should inspect the parade – which he did, riding on a white horse. Stalin stood on Lenin's mausoleum and watched. But within a year Zhukov had fallen from power. In a typical act of paranoid projection, at a Kremlin gathering at the end of 1945 Stalin accused Zhukov of taking the credit for all the war victories himself. Reports instigated by SMERSH denounced Zhukov, saying he was plotting to take power

Marshal Zhukov, on his famous white charger, inspects the victory parade in Red Square on 24 June 1945. By the end of the year this man, who had been the most effective Soviet commander of the war, would be in disgrace – accused, among other things, of 'taking too much credit' for the Soviet victory.

in a coup. Whilst Stalin did not imprison or torture Zhukov, he had him demoted and removed to command the Odessa military district far from Moscow and the centre of power. 'People at heart loved and supported Zhukov,' says Makhmud Gareev. 'But the situation did not allow them to express their protest. If someone had tried to say that Stalin was wrong, then this person would have been shut down immediately.'

Stalin ended the war much as he had begun it – with the tightest rein possible over his military commanders. Briefly, when it had been essential, he had listened to them and allowed them discretion; now all that was over. Soviet propaganda trumpeted that Stalin was the single genius who had won the greatest war in history. And, deprived of the true information, many believed it – even some of those to whom his harsh policies had brought nothing but suffering: 'He was our God,' says Tatiana Nanieva. 'Even when I was given a long prison sentence and branded a "Traitor of the Motherland" and punished to a lifetime exile, when Stalin died in 1953 I cried. I cried less when my own father died than when Stalin died. I couldn't imagine that we would be able to live without him. And when my fiancé came in – we weren't married yet – I asked him: 'How are we going to live? It's impossible without him!' He answered: "Calmly." He was cleverer than I was.'

OPPOSITE Red Army soldiers display captured German colours in Red Square. Now the war was over, it was time for Stalin to ensure that history was rewritten, his mistakes erased and his personal successes exaggerated.

REFERENCES

Sources are given here usually in an abbreviated form; for full titles see the Bibliography.

CHAPTER ONE

p. 13   at least 25 million... The number of Soviet citizens who died in the war is still in dispute. Before the fall of Communism, estimates were around 20 million. Now, one estimate is a total of 30 million dead, but others are still considerably lower. The lack of detailed records means that the exact number may never be known. Professor Overy quotes 25 million (*Russia's War*, p. 288), but this is now a relatively low estimate. Professor Robert Service quotes 26 million Soviet dead in his *History of Twentieth-century Russia*, and Professor John Erickson estimates 27 million.

p. 14   'We are taking...' Noakes and Pridham, Vol. 2, p. 281.

p. 14   'Judaeo-Bolshevist...' Cecil, p. 167.

p. 15   'Germany will...' Noakes and Pridham, Vol. 2, p. 278.

p. 15   'an uncivilized...' Domarus, Max, *Hitler: Speeches and Proclamations, Vol. 2, 1935–38* (I.B. Taurus, 1992); Nuremberg Party rally, 13 September 1937.

p. 15   'an inferior race...' Cecil, p. 15, from Rauschning, H., *Hitler Speaks* (Thornton Butterworth, 1939) p. 140.

p. 18   'unbelievably bloody...' Leach, p. 14.

p. 18   'The German forces...' Salisbury, p. 154.

p. 18   Halder described how... Halder, *Spruchkammeraussage,* 20 September 1948, IfZ ZS 240/6, pp. 23–4.

p. 19   'military intervention...' Burdick and Jacobsen, pp. 220–1.

p. 19   'It is thus...' Ibid., p. 446.

p. 19   'I will keep. ..' Letter from Franz Halder to Luise von Benda, 3 July 1941; BA-MA, N 124/5: Colonel J. Rohowsky (rtd) papers; private property Luise Jodl, née v. Benda.

p. 20   'man who got...' Suny, Ronald Grigor, 'Stalin and Stalinism 1930–53', Kershaw and Lewin, p. 30.

p. 20   'is unhappy because...' Ibid., p. 49.

p. 21   'All of us...' Talbott, Strobe (ed.) *Khrushchev Remembers*, (Deutsch, 1971), p. 307.

p. 21   'Being enormously...' *Trotsky Moyazhizn,* Vol. 2, pp. 213–14, quoted in Volkogonov, p. 57.

p. 21   'negative inspiration': Lewin, Moshe, 'Stalin in the Mirror of the Other', Kershaw and Lewin, p. 109.

p. 21   'we are forced...' Kershaw and Lewin, p. 124.

p. 24   'an enemy of...' A. A.Yepischev, as quoted in Volkogonov, p. 279.

p. 25 'Stalin is probably...' Reuth, Ralph (ed.), *Goebbels' Diaries* (Munich, 1990), Vol. 3, p. 198; 10 July 1937.

p. 25 For Hitler himself... With the notable exception of the Röhm Putsch of 1934, though that was directed at the Nazis' own SA – the brownshirts – and not the German Army. Ironically, Stalin, when he heard of the Röhm Putsch, remarked how much he approved of it.

p. 28 'The Soviet "mass"...' Bullock, *Hitler and Stalin, Parallel Lives*, p. 731.

p. 30 'forced to make...' Quoted in Fest, *Hitler*, p. 644.

p. 32 But the majority... See Christian Streit, 'The German Army and the Policies of Genocide' in Hirschfeld. In Streit's view, 'Statements by troop commanders that they had not passed it [the Commissar Order] on or had forbidden its execution prove to be wrong in most cases. Only in one instance do sources verify that a divisional commander ignored the order.'(p. 8).

p. 33 'The Führer says...' Elke Froehlich, *'Joseph Goebbels und sein Tagebuch'*, *Vierteljahrshefte für Zeitgeschichte*, 35, 1987.

p. 34 'Most of the people...' *Voenno-istoricheskii Zhurnal* No. 9, p. 49, 1987, quoted in Volkogonov, p. 37.

p. 44 one estimate is... Volkogonov, p. 369.

p. 46 'I am mentally...' Overy, p. 74.

p. 46 'much obsolete...' Erickson, *The Soviet High Command*, p. 574.

p. 46 The British War Office... Bullock, *Hitler and Stalin, Parallel Lives*, p. 768.

p. 52 And any peace... Barros and Grefor.

p. 54 'the Soviet government...' Sudoplatov, pp. 145–7.

p. 55 'Molotov described...' Volkogonov, p. 413.

p. 57 the terrifying statistic... But note that one estimate is that 600,000 Soviet POWs were handed over during the war to Heydrich's Einsatzkommandos under his instructions of 17 July 1941, giving 'guidelines for the cleansing of camps for Soviet POWs'. These went further than the Commissar Order and called for the 'liquidation' not just of suspected commissars, party and state officials, but also of 'intellectuals' in the camps. See Christian Streit, 'The German Army and the Policies of Genocide' in Hirschfeld. (Also note that the figure of 600,000 is the subject of dispute.).

p. 60 'be fed...' Minutes of a meeting of civilian and military officials, 2 May 1941. *Nuremberg Trial Files*, Vol. 31, p. 84, Document 2718-PS.

p. 60 'Political-Economic Guidelines...' Ibid., Vol. 36 pp. 135–57.

p. 63 'The Führer is...' Quoted in Aly, p. 201; *Goebbels' Diaries*, Reuth (ed.), Vol. 4, 1645.

p. 63 compelling military studies... Deutsch and Showalter.

p. 70 'would never...' Quoted in Overy, p. 94.

p. 70 'For all military...' Bullock, *Hitler and Stalin, Parallel Lives*, p. 811.

p. 73 'When we assembled...' *Voenno-istoricheskii Zhurnal*, No. 10, pp. 335–41, 1991.

CHAPTER TWO

p. 77 Around 13 million... The question of just how many civilians died is controversial. See Overy, p. 288. This estimate comes from detailed consultation with Professor John Erickson.

p. 80 'the greatest crisis...' Quoted in Fest, *Hitler*, p. 655.

p. 81 'Do you think...' Ibid. p. 654.

p. 81 'It is not machines...' Noakes and Pridham, Vol. 3, p. 739.

p. 83 Goebbels also recorded... *Goebbels' Diaries*, 20 and 21 March 1942.

p. 87 'It's inconceivable...' Trevor-Roper, *Hitler's Table Talk*, entry for 23 September 1941, p. 38.

p. 87 'The earth continues...' Ibid., entry for 23 September 1941, p. 38.

p. 88 'There's only one...' Ibid., entry for 17 October 1941, p. 69.

p. 89 'Both the Führer...' Mulligan, p. 11, from notes by Dr Werner Koeppen, 19 September 1941.

p. 90 'Were it not...' Quoted in Dallin, p. 163.

p. 90 'we are a master...' Koch speech, 5 March 1943, quoted in Mulligan, p. 68.

p. 90 'Ukrainian children...' Quoted in Wistrich, p. 142.

p. 91 'No sooner...' Trevor-Roper, *Hitler's Table Talk*, entry for 19 February 1942, p. 319.

p. 92 'If some idiot...' Ibid., entry for 22 July 1942, pp. 587–9.

p. 92 'German public health...' Bormann to Rosenberg, 23 July 1942, Document NO-1878, quoted in Dallin, p. 457.

p. 92 The administrators... For a full history of this row see Dallin, pp. 454-8.

p. 103 General Halder... See Christian Streit, 'Partisans-Resistance-Prisoners of War', in Wieczynski.

p. 106 'This partisan war...' Bullock, *Hitler and Stalin, Parallel Lives*, p. 824.

p. 107 The partisan movement... Armstrong, pp. 21–7.

p. 109 The actual number... Estimates provided by Colonel David Glantz. See Grenkevich.

p. 109 As a general rule... Timoshenko claimed when interviewed that, when possible, if there were a secure route through to Red Army lines, he would send German prisoners back. This should be treated with scepticism. For a partisan unit operating behind enemy lines, it must almost always have been easier just to kill the German POWs as he describes.

p. 109 Stalin himself... Quoted in Mulligan, p. 137.

p. 111 'I served with...' NKGB report 17 March 1945, Minsk Central Archive.

p. 113 A secret... Ukrainian Interior Ministry Procurator's Report sent to 1st Party Secretary of Ukraine, 15 February 1949. Central State Archive, Kiev.

p. 115 This plaintive letter... Kosyk, p. 621.

p. 115 'The fight against...' Ibid., p. 554.

p. 116 'If the population...' Quoted in Mulligan, p. 139.

p. 116 'only where...' Quoted in Ibid., p. 139.

p. 118 'approximately two to three thousand...' Quoted in Ibid., p. 142.

p. 119 We traced... Report (sent 3 January 1944) to Army Group Centre about Operation Otto begun in December 1943. (Source BA-MA, RH 19 II/242, Anlagen KTB HG Mitte, 1.1.–24.9.44; Bandenbekämpfung, 01/44–03/44)

p. 120 'You appear not to know...' Quoted in Mulligan, p. 143.

CHAPTER THREE

p. 135 He became one of... Overy, p. 160.

p. 143 `Today's conference...' Quoted in Cooper, *The German Army, 1933–1945*, p. 443.

p. 175 'in no position to...' Keegan, p. 104.

p. 185 'What hurts me...' Warlimont, pp. 303–6.

p. 186 Just over 90,000 ... Statistics quoted in Beevor, p. 415.

CHAPTER FOUR

p. 198 An idea of... Buogai, p. 64.

p. 201 Beria himself wrote... Knight, p. 127.

p. 201 'If you give consent...' Ibid., p. 127.

p. 203 'If a bullet strikes...' Burrin, p. 38.

p. 205 'The Jews, who control...' Braham, 'The Politics of Genocide', in Hirschfeld, p. 363.

p. 210 'In 1944 children were thrown...' Pressac, p. 177.

p. 211 'Nowhere else but in...' Maier, p. 82.

p. 212 'If you say...' Speech to generals in Sonthofen, 24 May 1944; translation from Padfield, p. 484.

p. 216 In a directive of 8 March... Quoted in Adair, p. 66.

p. 216 'Ninth Army stands...' General der Infanterie Hans Jordan, quoted in Ziemke, p. 316.

p. 218 'HQ Ninth Army...' Adair, p. 117.

p. 224 This wholly uncharacteristic ... These conclusions are based on the consultative work completed for the television series by Colonel David Glantz.

p. 225 'If the German people...' Hauner.

p. 230 'We lecture our soldiers...' Quoted in Overy, p. 261.

BIBLIOGRAPHY

A brief selection of useful books:

Adair, Paul, *Hitler's Greatest Defeat* (Arms and Armour Press, 1994)

Aly, Götz, *Final Solution* (Arnold, 1999)

Anders, W., *Hitler's Defeat in Russia* (Henry Regnery Co., Chicago, 1953)

Armstrong, John A., *Soviet Partisans in World War Two* (University of Wisconsin Press, 1964)

Barros, James and Grefor, Richard, *Double Deception: Stalin, Hitler and the Invasion of Russia* (Northern Illinois University Press, 1995)

Bartov, Omar, *The Eastern Front, 1941-1945: German Troops and the Barbarization of Warfare* (Macmillan, London, 1985)

Beevor, Antony, *Stalingrad* (Viking Press, 1998)

Bialer, S. (ed.), *Stalin and His Generals: Soviet Military Memoirs of World War Two* (Pegasus, New York, 1969)

Bloch, Michael, *Ribbentrop* (Bantam Press, 1992)

Boshyk, Y. (ed.) *Ukraine During World War II: History and its Aftermath* (Canadian Institute of Ukrainian Studies, University of Alberta, 1986)

Broszat, Martin, *The Hitler State* (Longman, 1981)

Browning, Christopher, *Ordinary Men* (HarperCollins, 1992)

Browning, Christopher, *The Path to Genocide* (Cambridge University Press, 1992)

Bullock, Alan, *Hitler, a Study in Tyranny* (revised edition, Odhams, 1964)

Bullock, Alan, *Hitler and Stalin, Parallel Lives* (HarperCollins, 1991)

Buogai, Nikolai, *The Deportation of Peoples in the Soviet Union* (Nova Science Publishers, 1996)

Burdick, Charles and Jacobsen, Hans-Adolf (eds), *The Halder War Diary 1939-1942* (Greenhill, 1988)

Burrin, Philippe, *Hitler and the Jews* (Edward Arnold, 1994)

Cecil, Robert, *Hitler's Decision to Invade the Soviet Union* (Davis-Poynter, 1975)

Conquest, Robert, *Stalin: Breaker of Nations* (Weidenfeld & Nicolson, 1991)

Cooper, Matthew, *The German Army, 1933-1945* (Macdonald & Jane's, 1978)

Cooper, Matthew, *The Phantom War: The German Struggle against the Soviet Partisans* (Macdonald & Jane's, 1979)

Dallin, Alexander, *German Rule in Russia 1941-1945* (2nd edition, Macmillan, London, 1981)

Deutsch, Harold C. and Showalter, Dennis E., (eds), *What If? Strategic Alternatives of WWII* (Emperor's Press, Chicago, 1997)

Erickson, John, *The Road to Stalingrad* (Weidenfeld & Nicolson, 1975)

Erickson, John, *The Soviet High Command*, (Macmillan, London, 1962)

Erickson, John, *The Road to Berlin: Stalin's War with Germany* (Weidenfeld & Nicolson, 1983)

Erickson, John, 'New Thinking on the Eastern Front in World War II', *Journal of Military History*, 56 (1992)

Fest, Joachim, *The Face of the Third Reich* (Penguin Books, 1972)

Fest, Joachim, *Hitler* (Harcourt Brace Jovanovich, 1974)

Glantz, David, *Soviet Military Deception in the Second World War* (Frank Cass, 1989)

Glantz, David, *The Military Strategy of the Soviet Union: A History* (Frank Cass, 1992)

Glantz, David, *When Titans Clashed: How the Red Army Stopped Hitler* (University Press of Kansas, 1995)

Grenkevich, Leonid, *The Soviet Partisan Movement 1941–1944*, ed. Glantz, David (Frank Cass, 1999)

Hauner, Milan, *Hitler – A Chronology of His Life and Time* (Macmillan Press, 1983)

Hirschfeld, Gerhard, *The German Army and the Policies of Genocide* (German Historical Institute and Allen & Unwin, 1988)

Jukes, G., *Hitler's Stalingrad Decisions* (University of California Press, 1985)

Keegan, John (ed.), *The Times Atlas of the Second World War* (Times Books, 1989)

Kershaw, Ian and Lewin, Moshe, *Stalinism and Nazism* (Cambridge University Press, 1997)

Kershaw, Ian, *Hitler 1889–1936, Vol. I, Hubris* (Allen Lane, 1998)

Knight, Amy, *Beria – Stalin's First Lieutenant* (Princeton University Press, 1993)

Kosyk, Wolodymyr, *The Third Reich and Ukraine* (Peter Lang, 1993)

Leach, Barry, *German Strategy against Russia, 1939-41* (Oxford University Press, 1973)

Lockner, Louis P. (trans. and ed.), *The Goebbels Diaries* (Hamish Hamilton, 1948)

Lucas, John, *War on the Eastern Front* (Greenhill, 1991)

Maier, S. Charles, *The Unmasterable Past* (Harvard University Press, 1997)

Mommsen, Hans, *From Weimar to Auschwitz* (Polity Press, 1991)

Mulligan, Timothy Patrick, *The Politics of Illusion and Empire* (Praeger, 1988)

Niepold, Gerd, *Mittlere Ostfront Juni, 1944* (Mittler & Sohn, 1985), translated as *Battle for White Russia: The Destruction of Army Group Centre, June, 1944* (Brassey, 1987)

Noakes, J. and Pridham, G. (eds), *Nazism: A Documentary Reader, 1919-45*, Vols. 1–4 (University of Exeter Press, 1983-98)

Overy, Richard, *Russia's War* (Allen Lane, 1998)

Padfield, Peter, *Himmler Reichsführer SS* (Macmillan, London, 1990)

Pressac, Jean-Claude, *Auschwitz: Technique and Operation of the Gas Chambers* (Beate Klarsfeld Foundation, New York, 1989)

Salisbury, H.E, *Marshal Zhukov's Greatest Battles* (Harper & Row, 1969)

Schlacks, Charles Jr (ed.), *Operation Barbarossa* (Salt Lake City, 1991)

Sereny, Gitta, *Albert Speer, His Battle with Truth* (Macmillan, London, 1995)

Service, Robert, *A History of Twentieth-century Russia* (Allen Lane, 1997)

Sudoplatov, Pavel, *Special Tasks* (Warner Books, 1995)

Trevor-Roper, H.R., *The Last Days of Hitler* (Macmillan, London, 1947)

Trevor-Roper, H.R., *Hitler's Table Talk* (Oxford University Press, 1988)

Volkogonov, Dmitri, *Stalin: Triumph and Tragedy* (Weidenfeld & Nicolson, 1991)

Warlimont, Gen. Walter, *Inside Hitler's Headquarters, 1939-45* (Presido Press, 1964; first published Bernard & Graefe Verlag, 1962)

Wieczynski, J. (ed.), *Operation Barbarossa* (Salt Lake City, 1993)

Wistrich, Robert S., *Who's Who in Nazi Germany* (Routledge, 1995)

Ziemke, Earl, *Stalingrad to Berlin: The German Defeat in the East* (US Army Historical Series, Office of the Chief of Military History, Washington DC, 1987)

NOTES ON EYE-WITNESSES

ISRAEL ABELESZ
Born in 1930, he was 14 years old when he and his family arrived in Auschwitz-Birkenau as a result of the German deportation of Hungarian Jews in the spring/summer of 1944. His mother, father and younger brother were immediately selected for the gas chambers – he survived only due to a combination of luck and personal tenacity.

KIRA PAVLOVNA ALLILUYEVA-POLITKOVSKAYA
Born in 1922, she was Stalin's niece, the daughter of Pavel Alliluyev, who was the brother of Stalin's second wife, Nadezhda Alliluyeva. After the suspected poisoning of her father in the Kremlin before the war, she and her mother were later arrested and she spent five and a half years in forced exile.

ALEKSEY BALDUEVICH BADMAEV
Born in 1924 of ethnic Kalmyk descent, he was called up in 1942 and fought on the Stalingrad front as a private in the 302nd Division of the 51st Army, receiving a medal for valour. When in hospital as a result of wounds received in battle, he was forcibly deported to a labour camp in Siberia as part of the general Kalmyk deportations of December 1943 to January 1944.

BERNHARD BECHLER
Born in 1911, between autumn 1940 and spring 1942 he was ADC to General Eugen Müller (General for 'special duties') who was in charge of the drafting and interpretation of the infamous Commissar Order. From March 1942 he was a captain in the 3rd Infantry Division within the 6th Army. He was captured at Stalingrad on 28 January 1943.

CARLHEINZ BEHNKE
Born in 1922, he joined the Hitler Youth in 1933 and volunteered for the Waffen SS in 1940. He fought from the beginning of the Barbarossa campaign, first as a private in ArtilleryRegiment 5 of the SS-Panzer Division Wiking and subsequently as a junior officer in an SS Police Grenadier Division.

GÜNTHER VON BELOW
Born in 1905, he entered the Reichswehr in 1925. He was Quartermaster of 4 Corps in the French campaign and subsequently a senior officer within the 6th Army at Stalingrad. From 1943 to 1955 he was a Soviet POW.

MAYA IANOVNA BERZINA
Born in 1910. Her father was a close collaborator of Lenin's and one of his first ambassadors. In 1938 her father was shot dead in the purges because he was a 'suspect' Lithuanian. She experienced the panic in Moscow in October 1941, and with her husband and young child fled by boat from Moscow's southern port.

ALEKSEY BRIS
Born in 1922 in the Ukraine. He worked as an interpreter for the Germans in Gorokhov

during their occupation of the Ukraine. In 1942, after witnessing the mistreatment of his fellow countrymen at the hands of the Germans, he joined the UPA – the Ukrainian Nationalist Partisans.

FYODOR VASILIEVICH BUBENCHIKOV

Born in 1916, he first saw action in the war as a commander of a penal battalion at the Battle of Kursk. He subsequently participated in Operation Bagration and was wounded at Danzig in early 1945.

ALBERT LVOVICH BURKOVSKI

Born in 1928 in Stalingrad, when the fighting started he was left alone in the city after his grandmother had been killed. He was adopted by the Soviet 13th Radimeev Division and personally killed Germans at close range on the Mamaev Kurgan.

HEINZ FIEDLER

Born in 1922, he was drafted into the Reiter-Regiment 10 in Torgau and trained as a radio operator. In the summer of 1944 he fought against the Red Army during their Bagration offensive and escaped from the fortified place of Bobruisk.

VENIAMIN POLIKARPOVICH FYODOROV

Born in 1924, he served as a private with the 77th Guards Infantry Regiment of the Red Army during Operation Bagration.

MARK LAZAREVICH GALLAY

Born in 1914, from 1936 he worked as a Soviet test pilot at the Central Aerodynamic Institute. During the late 1930s he witnessed the effect of the purges on Soviet military aviation.

MAKHMUD AKHMEDOVICH GAREEV

Born in 1923 of Tatar nationality, he served more than 50 years in the Red Army, finishing his service as Deputy Chief of the General Staff of the USSR Armed Forces. In 1942 he was a captain, commanding the 3rd Battalion of the 120 Infantry Brigade, and by 1944 he was a major, the Operations Officer in the Headquarters of 45 Infantry Corps.

INNA VLADIMIROVNA GAVRILCHENKO

Born in 1926, she lived through the German occupation of Kharkov, witnessing her own father's death from starvation in May 1942.

IVAN IVANOVICH GOLOKOLENKO

Born in 1921, he volunteered to fight in the war in June 1941. In the autumn of 1942, as a lieutenant in the 19th Tank Brigade of the 26th Tank Corps, he participated in the Soviet Operation Uranus.

PETER VON DER GROEBEN

Born in 1903, he was a senior German military officer during the war. In 1943–4 he was Chief of Operations of Army Group Centre, and he finished the conflict as Major General of the 3rd Cavalry Division.

ANATOLY MARKOVICH GUREVICH

Born in 1916, he was Head of Soviet Military Counter-intelligence in France and Belgium during World War II. During 1940 he learnt of the German intention to invade the Soviet Union and passed on the information to Moscow. At the end of 1942 he was arrested by the Gestapo. After the war he was accused by the NKVD and imprisoned for 12 years. He was 'rehabilitated' in 1991.

GERHARD HINDENLANG
Born in 1916, he began the Barbarossa campaign as a lieutenant with the 71st Infantry Division. By January 1943 he was a battalion commander at Stalingrad. From 1943 to 1950 he was a prisoner of war. He is a recipient of the German Cross in Gold, one of the highest awards in the German Army.

WOLFGANG HORN
Born in 1920, he was a junior NCO with the 10th Panzer Division, commanding a six-man gun crew. He took part in Army Group Centre's advance to Moscow and his unit reached to within 30 kilometres of the Russian capital.

TAMARA BATYRBEKOVNA KALMYKOVA
Born in 1925, she participated in the defence of Stalingrad as a communications officer with the Soviet 64th Army and was wounded in November 1942.

VLADIMIR KRISTAPOVICH KANTOVSKI
Born in 1923, he was sentenced to ten years' hard labour in 1941 for distributing leaflets protesting at the arrest of one of his school-teachers. In 1942 he volunteered for a penal battalion and served in the 54th Penal Company. He was severely wounded during his first attack. In 1944 he was arrested again and sentenced to six more years in the camps.

VALENTINA DMITRIEVNA KRUTOVA
Born in 1931, she was 11 years old when the Germans advanced on Stalingrad. Trapped within the German lines she, her younger sister and elder brother were lucky to survive after the death of their grandmother.

EVDOKIYA FYODOROVNA KUVAKOVA
Born in 1939, she was just four years old when the NKVD deported her and her family to Siberia as part of the punishment relocation of the Kalmyks.

MARIA MAUTH
Born in 1924, she served in the Reich Labour Service during the war.

WALTER MAUTH
Born in 1923, he served as a lance corporal in a heavy machine gun company of the 30th Infantry Division. During 1943 and 1944 he participated in the German 'scorched earth' retreat.

HUBERT MENZEL
Born in 1908, he joined the German Army in 1927. From April to October 1941 he participated in the planning and then the direction of Operation Barbarossa as a major in the Operations Department of OKH (Army High Command). In November 1942 he was appointed Chief of Operations (Ia) of the 16th Panzer Division in Stalingrad. From 1943 to 1955 he was a POW in Russia.

ANATOLY GRIGORIEVICH MERESHKO
Born in 1922, he was a committed member of the Communist Party and as a young officer fought against the Germans' Operation Blue and subsequently in the defence of Stalingrad. From then until the end of the war he was an officer 'for special tasks' in Chuikov's Headquarters. After the war he rose to become Deputy Military Commander of the Warsaw Pact.

ALEKSANDR ANDREEVICH MIKHAILOVSKI
Born in 1921. During an anti-partisan sweep which encompassed their village of Maksimovka in Belorussia, he and his deaf and dumb brother were made to walk down a road that the Germans suspected was mined.

STEPAN ANASTASEVICH MIKOYAN
Born in 1921, he was the eldest son of Politburo member Anastas Mikoyan. He grew up in the Kremlin compound, playing with Stalin's own children, and went to flying school with Stalin's son Vasilij. He served as a pilot during the war.

SUREN GAREGINOVICH MIRZOYAN
Born in 1923, from May 1942 he served as a private in a reconnaissance patrol with the 33rd Guards Rifle Division in the Soviet 62nd Army. He fought in the Caucasus, the Kalach area and at Stalingrad, and ended the war in the Ukraine.

GERHARD MÜNCH
Born in 1915, in 1941 he was adjutant of the 194th Infantry Regiment with the 71st Infantry Division. In 1942 his was the first German battalion to reach the Volga in Stalingrad. He was flown out of the Stalingrad encirclement on 22 January 1943. After the war he became a general in the West German Army.

TATIANA POLIKARPOVNA NANIEVA
Born in 1920, she was a field nurse on the south-western front and was captured in a German encirclement in 1942. After imprisonment in a number of German camps, she was 'liberated' by the Red Army in January 1945. Despite being a committed

Communist, she was then sentenced to six years in a labour camp, followed by lifelong exile in Siberia. But in June 1956 she was allowed back to the Ukraine and in 1958 she was 'rehabilitated'.

NADEZHDA VASILIEVNA NEFYODOVA
Born in 1927, she was 14 years old when the Germans over-ran her village of Usyazha, 50 kilometres east of Minsk in Belorussia. She and her family were trapped between the Germans (who killed her brother) and the Soviet partisans (who killed her sister).

VLADIMIR TIMOFEEVICH OGRYZKO
Born in 1917, by 1939 he was a junior officer with the NKVD Moscow Division. During the Moscow panic of October 1941, he commanded a secret police unit which helped restore order. In the winter of 1941 he also served alongside the backmarker divisions on the Moscow front as part of the 1st NKVD Division.

NIKONOR PETROVICH PEREVALOV
Born in 1917, in 1943 he was a junior lieutenant and commander of a snipers' platoon in the 22nd NKVD Rifle Regiment. In December 1943 he participated in the Kalmyk deportations.

NIKOLAY VASILIEVICH PONOMARIEV
Born in 1916, he was a communications officer in the General Staff Headquarters before the war, becoming Stalin's own personal telegraphist from July 1941 until the end of the war.

ZINAIDA GRIGORIEVNA PYTKINA

Born in 1921, she took part in the Stalingrad battle as a nurse with the 88th Tank Brigade. In 1943 she was selected to join SMERSH ('Death to Spies') as a lieutenant and counter-intelligence officer working alongside the Headquarters of the 54th Tank Brigade within the 3rd Tank Army.

RÜDIGER VON REICHERT

Born in 1917, he joined the Wehrmacht in 1936 and by 1941 was a battery commander in the 268th Infantry Division, 4th Army, Army Group Centre. By the end of the war he was a major on the General Staff. After the war he went on to become a general in the West German Army.

WALTRAUD RESKI

Born in 1934, she was 11 years old when the Red Army set fire to her home town of Demmin in East Germany in 1945. Her mother was repeatedly raped by Soviet soldiers.

ANATOLY IVANOVICH REVA

Born in 1935, he was six years old when the Germans occupied the eastern Ukrainian city of Kharkov. With his father dead and his mother in hospital he roamed the streets before being placed in an orphanage, where he nearly died of starvation.

WALTER SCHAEFER-KEHNERT

Born in 1918, he was an artillery officer with the 11th Panzer Division fighting in Kiev, Uman, Vyazma and Moscow. His unit was sent to France in May 1944.

ALBERT SCHNEIDER

Born in 1923, he was a mechanic with the 201st Assault Gun Battalion, fighting through Minsk, Borisov, Smolensk and Orsha to within 30 kilometres of Moscow. In 1942 he was transferred to the 101st Artillery Battalion and deployed near Stalingrad.

GEORGY VALERIEVICH SEMENYAK

Born in 1921, he was a scout with the 204th Division within the 11th Mechanized Corps. He began the war in Belorussia and was taken prisoner by the Germans on 6 July 1941 near Minsk. He was one of the few Soviet prisoners captured so early in the war to survive German captivity. After the war, and throughout his working life, he suffered discrimination within the Soviet state because he had been taken prisoner.

MELETI SEMENYUK

Born in 1912, he lived in a small hamlet near Gorokhov in the Ukraine. During the war he joined the UPA (the Ukrainian Nationalist Partisans) fighting both the Germans and the Soviet partisans.

VLADIMIR EFIMOVICH SEMICHASTNY

Born in the Ukraine in 1924, he was a member of the Komsomol during the war and became head of the KGB in 1961.

JOACHIM STEMPEL

Born in 1920, in 1941 he was a lieutenant with the 108th Panzer Grenadier Regiment within the 14th Panzer Division. He was caught within the Stalingrad encirclement, where his own father (a general and a divisional commander) committed suicide. From 1943 to 1949 he was a POW in the Soviet Union.

VIKTOR ADOLFOVICH STRAZDOVSKI

Born in 1923, he volunteered for the Red Army in 1941. As a private in the 52nd Infantry Regiment, 18th Division, 32nd Army, he fought at the Battle of Vyazma and subsequently at Stalingrad and Kursk.

FYODOR DAVIDOVICH SVERDLOV

Born in 1921, he commanded an infantry company with the 19th Infantry Brigade, 49th Army. In the winter of 1941 he and his men fought in the area of Kubinki during the defence of Moscow.

VERA BADMAEVNA TACHIEVA

Born in 1924, in January 1944 she was studying at a teacher training college on the Kalmyk steppe when she and her fellow students were suddenly deported to Siberia by the NKVD as part of the action against the Kalmyks.

WILHELM TER-NEDDEN

Born in 1904, he joined the Nazi Party in 1937. From the summer of 1941 he was Deputy Head of Economic Staff East. He also worked in Rosenberg's Ministry for the Occupied Eastern Territories. During the German occupation of the Ukraine, he witnessed the acrimonious relationship between Rosenberg and Koch.

MIKHAIL IVANOVICH TIMOSHENKO

Born in 1909, he took part in the Finnish war with the 44th Ukrainian Division. In June 1941 he and his NKVD comrades fruitlessly tried to resist the initial German assault on the Soviet border. Later in 1941 he was the political commissar of a partisan unit behind the German lines.

WALTER TRAPHÖNER

Born in 1908, he served as a private (subsequently lance corporal) with an SS cavalry regiment operating in the rear of Army Group Centre. He was wounded in December 1942 and sent back to Germany.

IVAN STEPANOVICH TRESKOVSKI

Born in 1928, he lived in Usyazha, 50 kilometres east of Minsk in Belorussia. Like his fellow villager, Nadezhda Vasilievna Nefyodova, he experienced the brutality of both the Germans and the Soviet partisans.

BORIS VLADIMIROVICH VITMAN

Born in 1920, he served as an intelligence officer at the Headquarters of 6th Army on the south-western front. He fought in the ill-fated Kharkov advance of May 1942 and was taken prisoner by the Germans during the Barvenkovo encirclement.

HELMUT WALZ

Born in 1922, he was a private with the 305th Infantry Division and fought hand-to-hand with Red Army soldiers in Stalingrad in October 1942. He was severely wounded on 17 October and spent the rest of the war in hospital.

ACKNOWLEDGEMENTS

There are many people I need to thank.

The enthusiasm of Mark Thompson, then Controller of BBC2, made this project possible in the first place. His successor, Jane Root, has been just as supportive, as has Paul Hamann, Head of Documentaries and History. Professor Ian Kershaw carried on to this series the invaluable role he performed on *The Nazis: A Warning from History* as series historical and script consultant. Other academics were also extremely helpful: in Britain, Professor Robert Service and Professor John Erickson; in the United States, Colonel David Glantz; in Russia, Professor Vladimir Naumov, Dr Kirill Anderson, General Yuri Gorkov, Dr Sergey Sluch, Dr Svetlana Argasceva, Professor Alexander Chubarian and Nikita Petrov; in Belorussia, Professor Aleksei Litvin; in the Ukraine, Dr Sergei Kot and Dr Yuri Shapoval; in Germany, Dr Volker Rieß, Dr Christian Gerlach, Andrej Angrick and Peter Klein.

Since this book is based on a television series, it is only proper that I also thank the production team of *War of the Century*. Detlef Siebert was the series associate producer, and without his fine journalism the programmes – and this book – would have been immensely poorer. His commitment to the project was unswerving, his judgement immaculate. The assistant producers were Martina Balazova, Tomasz Lasica and Alexandra Umminger; all did first-rate work. Stuart Russell, Manfred Oldenburg, Marcel Joos and Frank Stucke also did important research for us in Germany. In Russia, Elena Yakovleva, Maria Keder, Elena Smolina, Stanislav Remizov, Eric Shur, Valeri Azarianc, Anya Narinskaya, Maria Razumovskaya, Maria Mikushova, Valentina Galzanova, Teodor Matveev and Viktor Belyakov all made an essential contribution, as did Roksolyana and Taras Shumeiko in the Ukraine. The camera crew of Martin Patmore and Brian Biffin cheerfully criss-crossed the former Soviet Union with me, often in trying circumstances. Katherine Manners travelled the world finding archive film for us, and Joanne King did the same marvellous job on stills research as on the previous series; she also researched the photographs for this book. John Kennedy made another vital artistic contribution to the series with his graphic design, and Alan Lygo was the film editor – it is no accident that he is the only practitioner of his craft ever to win three separate BAFTA awards for his work. Without Kate Gorst as production assistant, Ann Cattini and Shirley Escott as unit managers and Tanya Batchelor as my own assistant, the production would have ground to a halt.

Once again, it is important I record the vital contribution made to this series by our American co-producers – A&E/the History Channel. I remain profoundly grateful to Charlie Maday, Abbe Raven, Joseph La Polla, Michael Cascio and Brooke Johnson for their continued support. The creative contribution they have made to serious historical journalism over the years is enormous.

I was also fortunate that Volker Zielke at NDR was enthusiastic about the project from the first and I benefited greatly from his advice. I am proud to have such a distinguished European programme-maker as another co-producer.

At BBC Worldwide Anna Ottewill and Martha Caute were always encouraging. Andrew Nurnberg was also a great help at steering this book through foreign waters.

Of course, I also thank our many interviewees, whose names I have recorded in this book in the section Notes on Eye-witnesses. The hospitality they showed to us, particularly in the former Soviet Union, was at times overwhelming.

A number of people read this book in draft form, including my wife Helena, Detlef Siebert, Professor Kershaw and Professor Service. I am grateful to them all for their comments. But notwithstanding the galaxy of experts whom I have had the privilege of consulting, the opinions and judgements in this book are my own.

LR

INDEX

PICTURE CREDITS